EYEWITNESS
KNIGHT

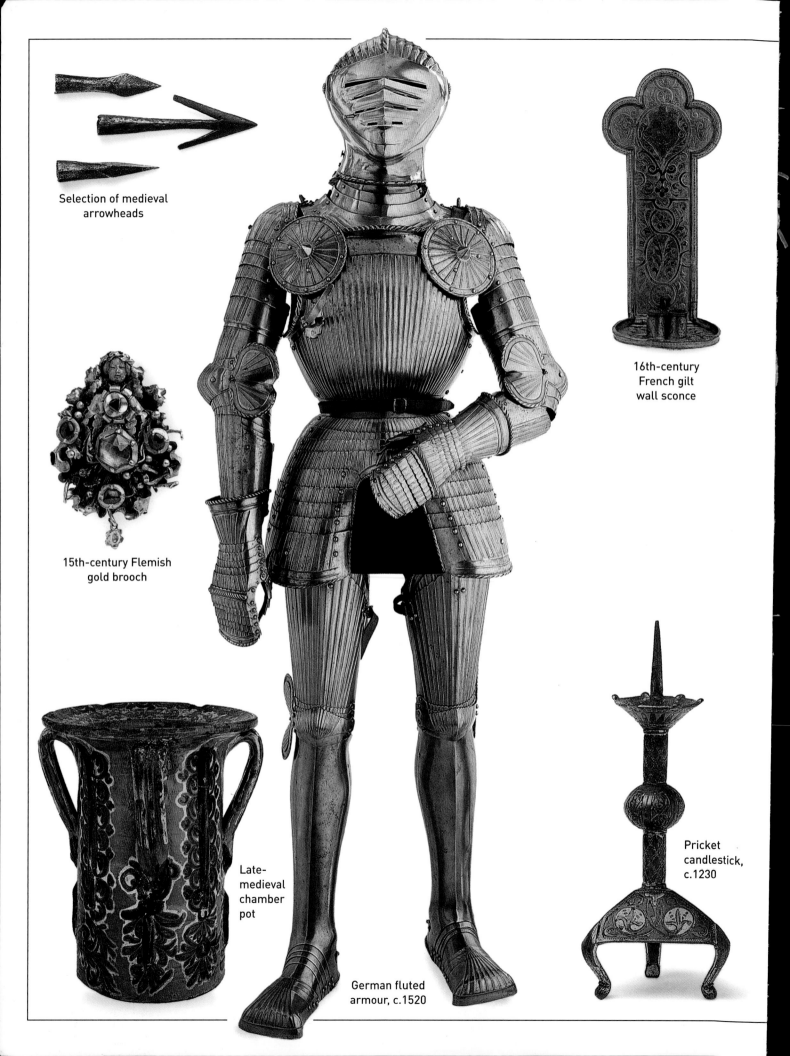

Selection of medieval arrowheads

16th-century French gilt wall sconce

15th-century Flemish gold brooch

Late-medieval chamber pot

German fluted armour, c.1520

Pricket candlestick, c.1230

EYEWITNESS
KNIGHT

Written by
CHRISTOPHER GRAVETT

Photographed by
GEOFF DANN

15th-century
German
serving knife

16th-century Italian parade helmet

Late 16th-century
German halberd

15th-century
Flemish shaffron

Plaque showing a knight
on horseback

15th-century
Italian barbute

15th-century
spur

DK | Penguin
Random
House

Project editor Phil Wilkinson

Art editor Ann Cannings
Managing editor Helen Parker
Managing art editor Julia Harris
Production Louise Barratt
Picture research Kathy Lockley

RELAUNCH EDITION (DK UK)
Senior editor Chris Hawkes
Senior art editor Spencer Holbrook
Jacket editor Claire Gell
Jacket designer Laura Brim
Jacket design development manager Sophia MTT
Producer, pre-production Francesca Wardell
Producer Janis Griffith
Managing editor Linda Esposito
Managing art editor Philip Letsu
Publisher Andrew Macintyre
Publishing director Jonathan Metcalf
Associate publishing director Liz Wheeler
Design director Stuart Jackman

RELAUNCH EDITION (DK INDIA)
Project editor Bharti Bedi
Project art editor Nishesh Batnagar
DTP designer Pawan Kumar
Senior DTP designer Harish Aggarwal
Picture researcher Nishwan Rasool
Jacket designer Suhita Dharamjit
Managing jackets editor Saloni Talwar
Pre-production manager Balwant Singh
Managing editor Kingshuk Ghoshal
Managing art editor Govind Mittal
First published in Great Britain in 1993
This revised edition published in Great Britain in 2007, 2015
by Dorling Kindersley Limited,
80 Strand, London WC2R ORL

Copyright © 1993, 2007, 2015 Dorling Kindersley Limited
A Penguin Random House Company

10 9 8 7 6 5 4 3 2 1
280093 – Jun/15

ISBN 978-0-2411-8762-3

Printed by South China Printing Co. Ltd., China

Discover more at
www.dk.com

German
halberd,
c.1500

16th-
century
German
sword

Contents

Italian 16th-century
close-helmet for tilting

The first knights

In the fourth century CE barbarian tribes invaded the Roman Empire and Europe. A group called the Franks expanded their power, and in 800 CE their leader, Charlemagne, became Emperor of the West. In the ninth century, this empire broke up into smaller pieces, and powerful lords and their mounted warriors offered protection to peasants, who, in return, became their serfs. These lords, and some of the men who served them, were knights – warriors who fought on horseback. By the 11th, century a new social order was formed by armoured knights who served a local lord, count, or duke.

Winged spear
Infantrymen (foot soldiers) of Charlemagne (left) usually carried spears with sticking-out lugs (right); cavalrymen (mounted warriors) might have used smaller versions as well. The lugs prevent the spear getting stuck in an opponent's body.

Carolingian cavalry
Under Charlemagne and his sons (the Carolingians), armoured horsemen became increasingly important. In this ninth-century manuscript (above), the men have coats of scale armour, helmets, shields, and spears.

Sharp, double-edged blade

Lug

Socket to insert shaft

Barbarian horseman
When the Roman Empire broke up, many horsemen from eastern Europe arrived in the west. This plaque shows a Lombard horseman, who were the forerunners of the mounted warriors of later centuries.

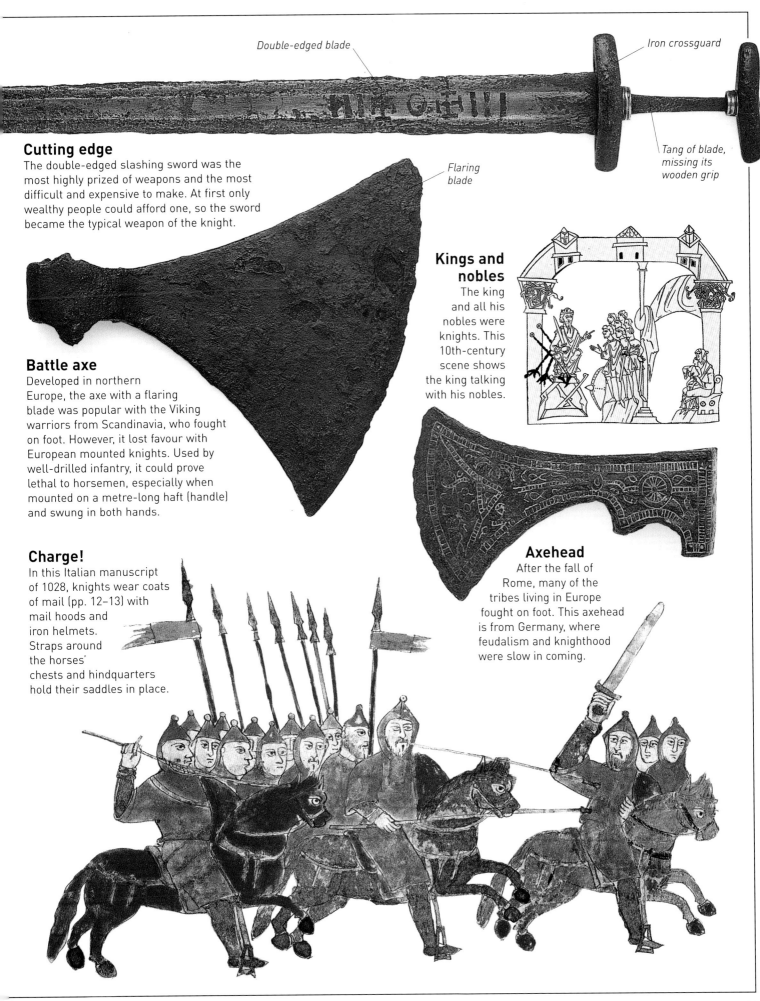

Double-edged blade

Iron crossguard

Tang of blade, missing its wooden grip

Cutting edge

The double-edged slashing sword was the most highly prized of weapons and the most difficult and expensive to make. At first only wealthy people could afford one, so the sword became the typical weapon of the knight.

Flaring blade

Battle axe

Developed in northern Europe, the axe with a flaring blade was popular with the Viking warriors from Scandinavia, who fought on foot. However, it lost favour with European mounted knights. Used by well-drilled infantry, it could prove lethal to horsemen, especially when mounted on a metre-long haft (handle) and swung in both hands.

Kings and nobles

The king and all his nobles were knights. This 10th-century scene shows the king talking with his nobles.

Axehead

After the fall of Rome, many of the tribes living in Europe fought on foot. This axehead is from Germany, where feudalism and knighthood were slow in coming.

Charge!

In this Italian manuscript of 1028, knights wear coats of mail (pp. 12–13) with mail hoods and iron helmets. Straps around the horses' chests and hindquarters hold their saddles in place.

The Normans

In an attempt to stop the Vikings raiding his territory, Charles III of France gave some land to a group of them in 911. Their new home was called Normandy, and their leader, Rollo, became its first duke. The Vikings fought on foot, but the Normans, as they became known, copied the French use of mounted knights. After the Battle of Hastings in 1066, Duke William of Normandy brought the knight, his castle, and the feudal system to England.

Metal boss

Seaborne army
Grim-faced armoured soldiers with spears and kite-shaped wooden shields stand ready on the deck of a ship. This French manuscript of the 11th century shows vessels like those used by the Normans to bring their invading army to England.

Prick

Leather straps were originally attached here

Prick spur
This 11th-century prick spur is made from tinned iron. It was fastened to the knight's foot by straps riveted to its arms.

Arm

Shielded from danger
This small 12th-century bronze figurine shows how knightly equipment slowly changed after the Norman conquest of England. The top of the helmet is tilted slightly forward, and the shield has a decorative metal boss in the centre.

Position of band to attach strap

Mouthpiece

Double-edged cutting blade

Riding to the attack
The above scene is from the Bayeux Tapestry, an embroidery made within 20 years of the Battle of Hastings. It shows Norman knights carrying shields, swords, and light lances. The small flags, called pennons, show them to be of high rank.

Shield wall

In this scene from the Bayeux Tapestry, the English defend their hilltop position at Hastings. Unlike the Normans, the English fought wholly on foot. The weapons of the higher-ranking troops are similar to those of the Normans, except for the large two-handed axe at the shoulder of the figure second to left. Bundles of javelins and a flying mace can also be seen.

Solid faith

The Normans used stone to build some of their castles (pp. 22–23), large cathedrals, abbeys, and churches throughout the newly conquered English kingdom. They used the Romanesque style of architecture, which included large columns and rounded arches, seen here in the nave of Durham Cathedral.

Nobbler

The surface of this 12th-century bronze mace could break an opponent's bones under flexible mail.

Moulded, nobbly protrusion could pierce mail

Carving of mythical beasts

Charioteer

Wrestlers

Battle horn

Horns were used not only to make music and announce dinner, but for signalling on the battlefield. This one was made in the 11th century from an elephant's tusk and comes from southern Italy. The Normans settled much of this area and conquered Sicily.

Cutting edge

This double-edged sword has a groove, called a fuller, running down the blade to make it lighter. The pommel helps to counter the weight of the blade, so the sword is easier to handle.

Fuller *Crossguard* *Pommel*

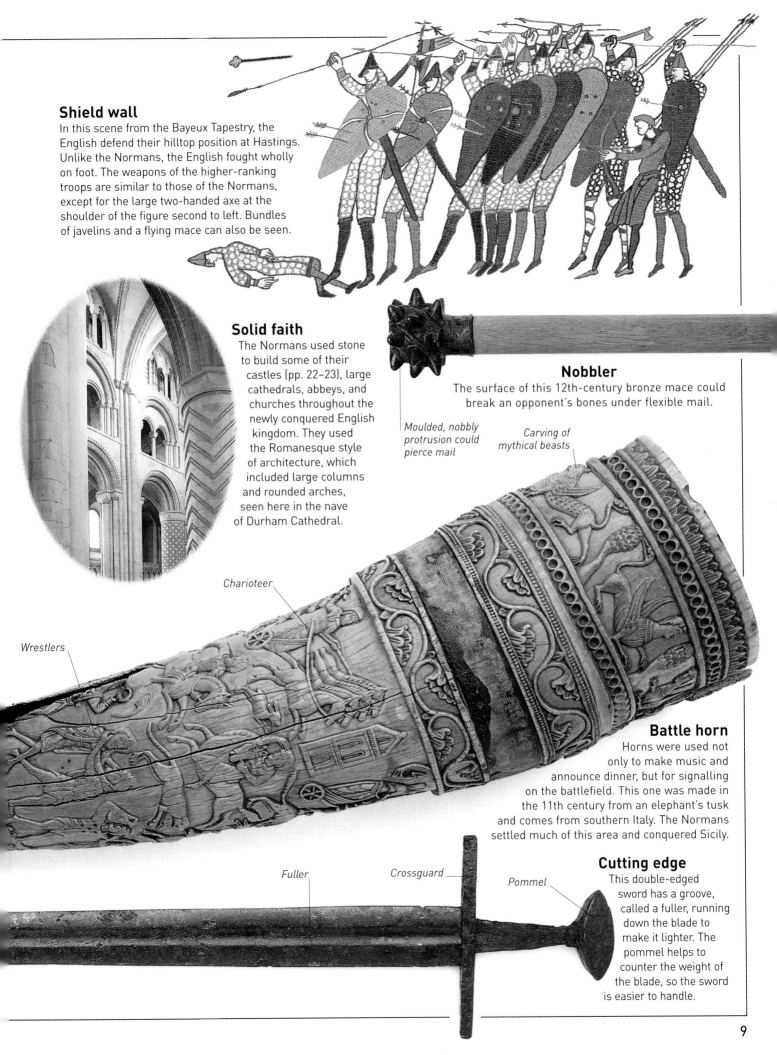

Making a knight

A boy of noble birth who was going to become a knight was usually sent away at age seven to a nobleman's household to be a page. Here he learned how to behave and how to ride a horse. When about 14, he was apprenticed to a knight whom he served as a squire and was taught how to handle weapons, and even went into battle with the knight to assist him. Successful squires were knighted when they were around 21 years old.

Backplate

Breastplate

Boy's cuirass
These pieces of armour from about 1600 are specially made to fit a boy. Only rich families could afford to give their young sons such a gift.

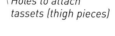
Holes to attach tassets (thigh pieces)

The page
Sons of noble families who were sent away to become a page learned a variety of skills, from serving a knight to the art of courtly manners and good breeding.

Practice makes perfect
Squires who wanted to be knights trained constantly to exercise their muscles and improve their skill with weapons. Such training was hard and not everyone could manage it. Those who did, eventually went on to become knights. This 15th-century picture shows various ways the young men could train.

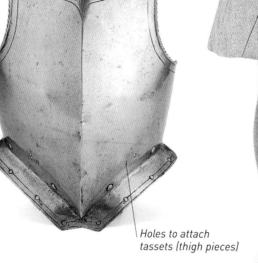

Putting the stone

Throwing the javelin

Acrobatics

Fighting with sword and buckler

Fighting with quarterstaff

Wrestling

The squire

In the 11th and 12th centuries, many squires were servants of a lower social class, but later the sons of noble families would become squires before being knighted. In the 13th century, becoming a knight was so expensive that many young men remained squires. Later the word squire came to mean a gentleman who owned land.

Chaucer's squire

Geoffrey Chaucer wrote his *Canterbury Tales* in about 1387. One of the stories is told by a squire, as seen above, who is the son of a knight and about 20 years old. He could compose songs, dance, draw, and write, and was also a good rider and knew how to joust. However, some other stories depict squires as thugs.

At the pel

Squires could practise against a wooden post, or pel. Sometimes they were given weapons double the weight to develop their muscles.

Clean cut

Chaucer notes how the squire carved the meat – an important skill – in front of his father at the dining table.

Thigh-length leather boots

Jousting practice

After striking the shield of a wooden structure, sometimes shaped like a soldier (above), the rider had to pass by quickly to avoid the swinging weight.

Dubbing

A squire was finally made into a knight at the ceremony of dubbing. This was originally a blow to the neck with the hand, though by the 13th century this had been replaced by a tap with the sword. The knight's sword and spurs were fastened on and celebrations might follow when he could show off his skills. Another knight, often the squire's master or the king, performed the dubbing.

Armour

Early knights wore armour made of small, linked iron rings called mail. During the 12th century knights started to wear more mail. In the 14th century knights added steel plates to protect their limbs, and the body was protected further with a coat-of-plates made of pieces of iron riveted to a cloth covering. By the 15th century some knights wore full suits of plate armour. A suit weighed about 20–25 kg (44–55 lb), and the weight was spread over the body so that a fit man could run, lie down, or mount a horse unaided.

Mail
Weighing about 9–14 kg (20–31 lb), most of the mail coat's weight was on the knight's shoulders. Each open ring is interlinked with four others and closed with a rivet.

Knightly plaque
This mounted knight from the 14th century has a helm fitted with a crest that identified him in battle. However, at this time, the basinet and visor was becoming popular.

Mail-maker
This 15th-century picture shows an armourer using pliers to join the links. He could shape the mail by increasing or reducing the number of links.

Pin allowing visor to be removed

Cord allowing mail to be removed

Basinet
This 14th-century Italian basinet was originally fitted with a visor that pivoted over the brow. But, at some point, a side-pivoting visor was fitted.

Ventilation holes

Modern mail neck guard

Courtly gauntlets
Gauntlet plates, like this late 14th-century pair from Milan, Italy, were riveted to a leather glove. Small plates were added to protect the fingers.

Sallet
Light horsemen often wore helmets like this German sallet of 1480–1510.

Visor with horizontal sight

Barbute
Italian barbutes, like this one of about 1445, were padded inside. Rivets lower down originally held a leather chin strap to stop the helmet being knocked off.

"Gothic-style" fluted decoration

Pointed cuff

Centre plate

Articulated plates

Shaped knuckle plate

Gauntlet
This German "Gothic" armour from the late 15th century gave better protection than mail because it was solid and did not flex when struck heavily by a weapon, such as a mace or sword.

Plate armour
The knight on the left, from about 1340, wears plate armour only on his legs. The knight on the right dates from about 1420 and has full plate armour.

Unhorsed
This 13th-century picture shows the large shields that knights used to protect themselves. By 1400, thanks to plate armour, shields had become much smaller.

The mailed knight
This knight from about 1250 wears a cloth surcoat over his mail, perhaps in imitation of Muslim dress seen on crusade.

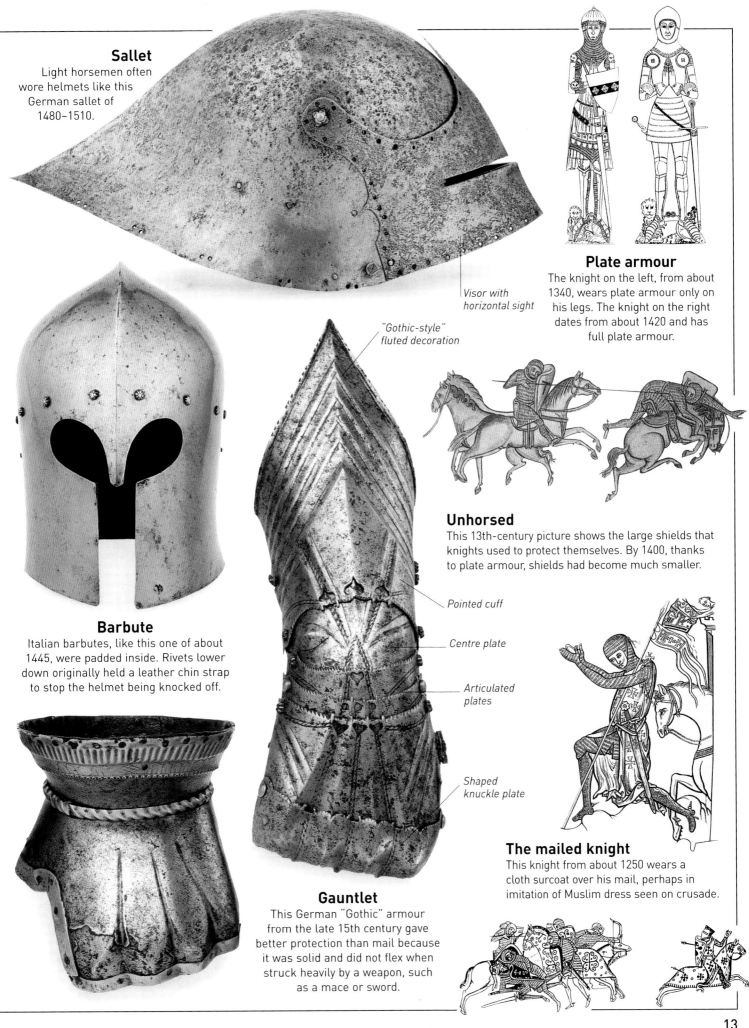

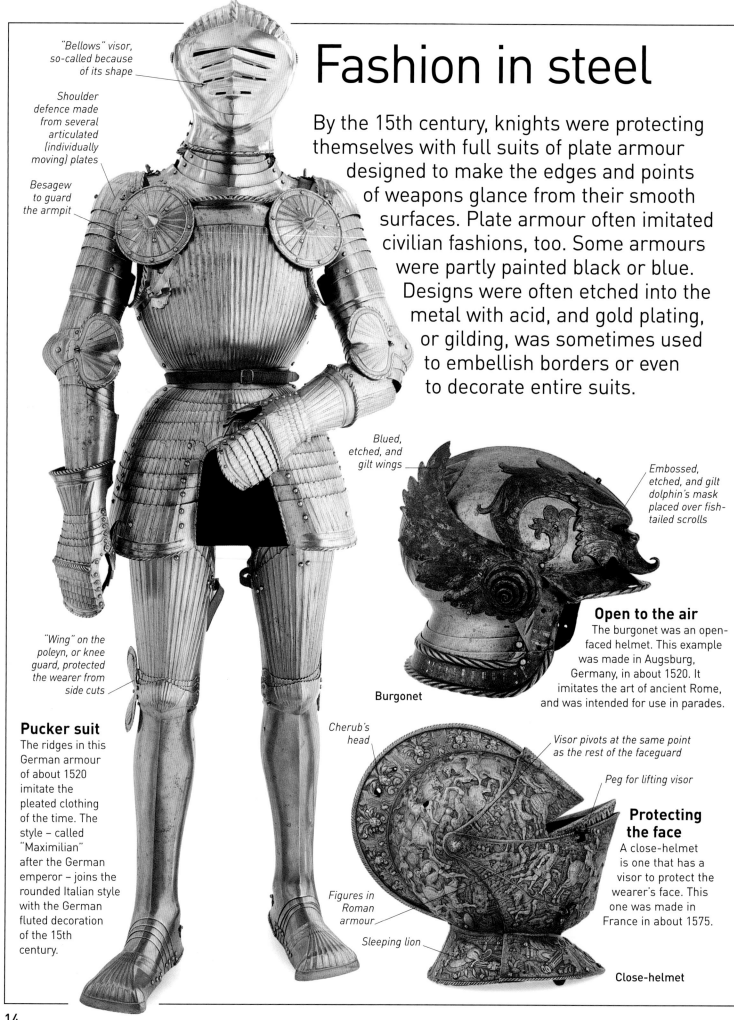

Fashion in steel

By the 15th century, knights were protecting themselves with full suits of plate armour designed to make the edges and points of weapons glance from their smooth surfaces. Plate armour often imitated civilian fashions, too. Some armours were partly painted black or blue. Designs were often etched into the metal with acid, and gold plating, or gilding, was sometimes used to embellish borders or even to decorate entire suits.

"Bellows" visor, so-called because of its shape

Shoulder defence made from several articulated (individually moving) plates

Besagew to guard the armpit

"Wing" on the poleyn, or knee guard, protected the wearer from side cuts

Pucker suit
The ridges in this German armour of about 1520 imitate the pleated clothing of the time. The style – called "Maximilian" after the German emperor – joins the rounded Italian style with the German fluted decoration of the 15th century.

Blued, etched, and gilt wings

Embossed, etched, and gilt dolphin's mask placed over fish-tailed scrolls

Burgonet

Open to the air
The burgonet was an open-faced helmet. This example was made in Augsburg, Germany, in about 1520. It imitates the art of ancient Rome, and was intended for use in parades.

Cherub's head

Visor pivots at the same point as the rest of the faceguard

Peg for lifting visor

Protecting the face
A close-helmet is one that has a visor to protect the wearer's face. This one was made in France in about 1575.

Figures in Roman armour

Sleeping lion

Close-helmet

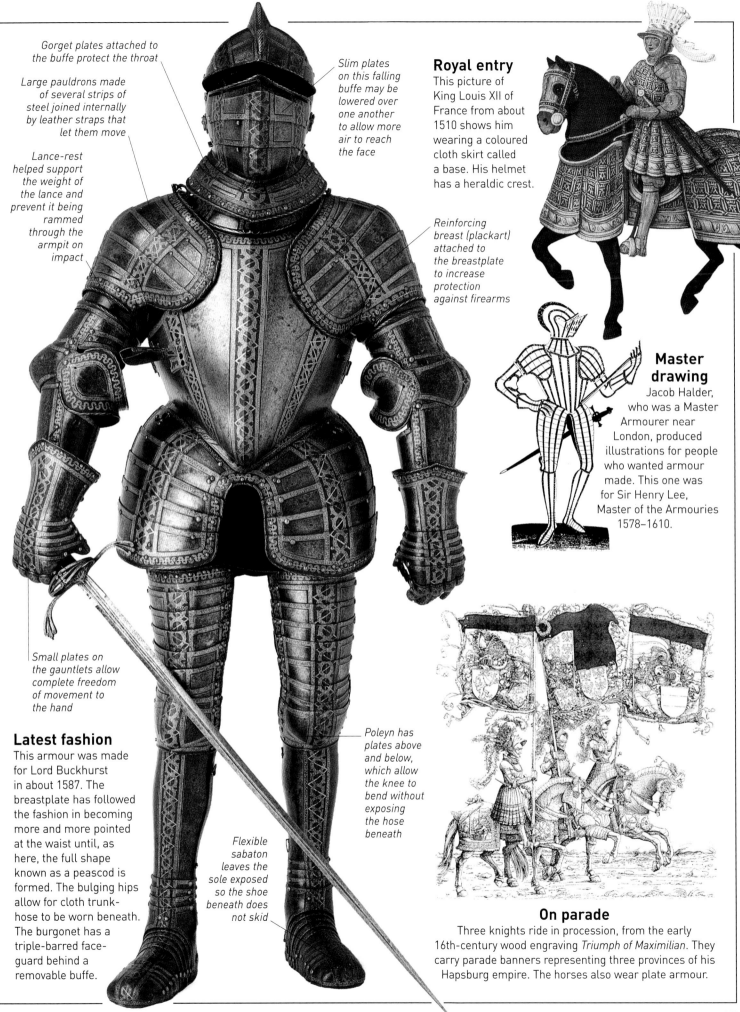

Gorget plates attached to the buffe protect the throat

Large pauldrons made of several strips of steel joined internally by leather straps that let them move

Lance-rest helped support the weight of the lance and prevent it being rammed through the armpit on impact

Slim plates on this falling buffe may be lowered over one another to allow more air to reach the face

Royal entry
This picture of King Louis XII of France from about 1510 shows him wearing a coloured cloth skirt called a base. His helmet has a heraldic crest.

Reinforcing breast (plackart) attached to the breastplate to increase protection against firearms

Master drawing
Jacob Halder, who was a Master Armourer near London, produced illustrations for people who wanted armour made. This one was for Sir Henry Lee, Master of the Armouries 1578–1610.

Small plates on the gauntlets allow complete freedom of movement to the hand

Latest fashion
This armour was made for Lord Buckhurst in about 1587. The breastplate has followed the fashion in becoming more and more pointed at the waist until, as here, the full shape known as a peascod is formed. The bulging hips allow for cloth trunk-hose to be worn beneath. The burgonet has a triple-barred face-guard behind a removable buffe.

Flexible sabaton leaves the sole exposed so the shoe beneath does not skid

Poleyn has plates above and below, which allow the knee to bend without exposing the hose beneath

On parade
Three knights ride in procession, from the early 16th-century wood engraving *Triumph of Maximilian*. They carry parade banners representing three provinces of his Hapsburg empire. The horses also wear plate armour.

Inside the armour

A man in armour could do just about anything a man can do when not wearing it. Some plates were attached to each other with a rivet, which allowed the two parts to pivot at that point. Others were joined by a sliding rivet, so the two plates could move in and out. Tubular-shaped plates could also have a sticking-up, or flanged, edge to fit inside the edge of another tubular plate so that they could twist around.

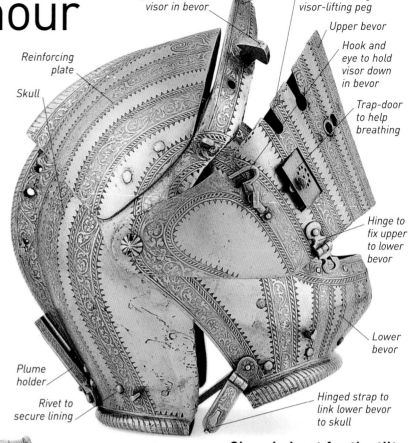

Key to lock down visor in bevor

Visor

Slot for missing visor-lifting peg

Upper bevor

Hook and eye to hold visor down in bevor

Trap-door to help breathing

Reinforcing plate

Skull

Hinge to fix upper to lower bevor

Lower bevor

Plume holder

Rivet to secure lining

Hinged strap to link lower bevor to skull

Close helmet for the tilt
This Italian helmet of about 1570 has a reinforcing plate riveted to the skull. The visor fits inside the bevor, which is divided into two parts.

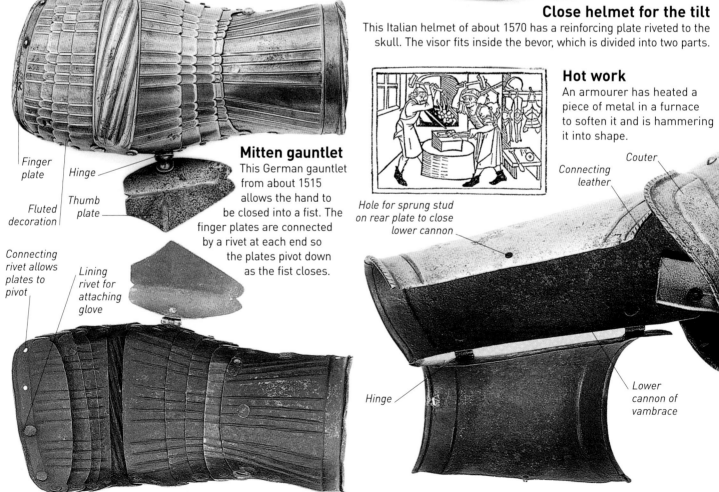

Finger plate

Hinge

Fluted decoration

Thumb plate

Mitten gauntlet
This German gauntlet from about 1515 allows the hand to be closed into a fist. The finger plates are connected by a rivet at each end so the plates pivot down as the fist closes.

Connecting rivet allows plates to pivot

Lining rivet for attaching glove

Hole for sprung stud on rear plate to close lower cannon

Hot work
An armourer has heated a piece of metal in a furnace to soften it and is hammering it into shape.

Couter

Connecting leather

Hinge

Lower cannon of vambrace

Roped inward turn

Recessed border

Medial rib

Poleyn

Roped rib

Pierced hole for stud of lower leg defence

Cuisse

Wing to guard against side cuts

Rivet for internal strap

Rivet allows plates to pivot

Side wing

Keyhole slot to attach stud of lower leg defence

Modern replacement tab to lace to torso

Cuisse and poleyn

This is a 16th-century defence for the thigh (cuisse) and knee (poleyn) of the right leg. The back of the thigh was usually left unprotected. The cuisse is laced to the wearer's torso, and holes at the lower edge take studs that stick out from the lower leg armour.

Modern leather strap to buckle around thigh

Inside of cuisse

Buckle to fasten poleyn around back of knee

Connecting leather

Modern strap

Shaping up

This 16th-century armourer is shaping cold metal using an anvil. He would also place the metal on a tree trunk while hammering it.

Upper cannon of vambrace

Turner

Sliding rivet

Articulating rivet

Pauldron

Pauldron and vambrace

This 16th-century right-arm defence protects the whole arm. The shoulder defence (pauldron) is made of several plates (lames) connected by sliding rivets and internal leathers, so they can all move over one another. The pauldron is connected to the upper arm (vambrace) by a turner, which allows the arm to twist outwards.

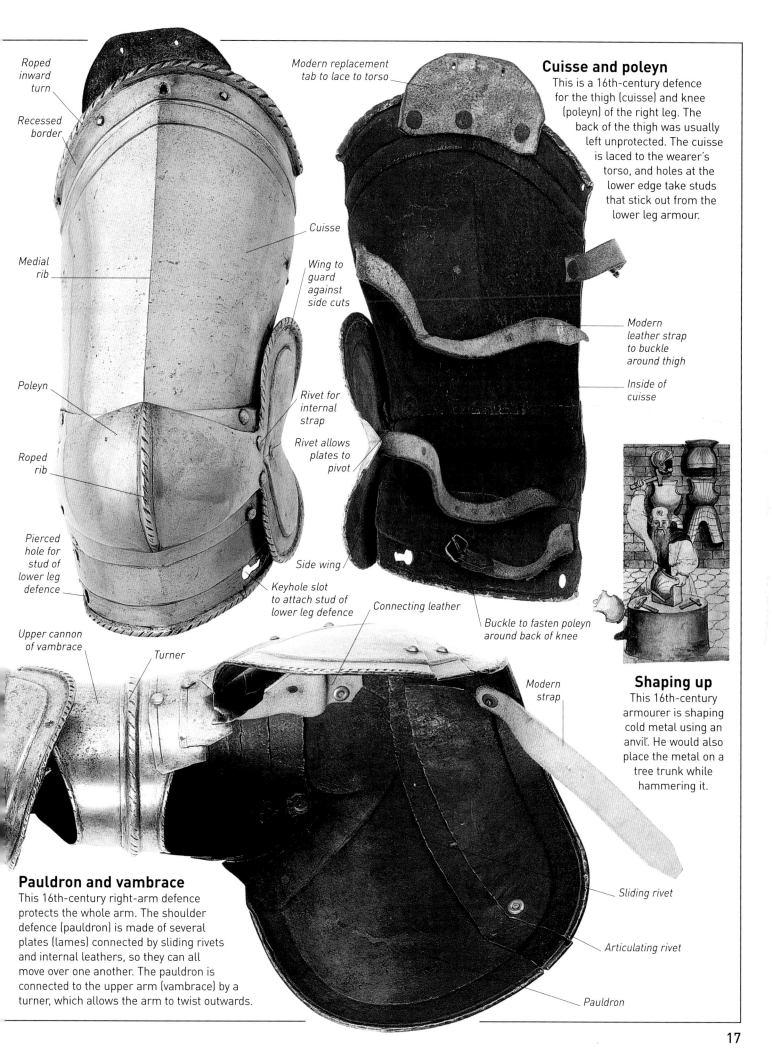

Arms and the man

The sword was the most important knightly weapon. As plate armour became more common, pointed swords became popular than the double-edged cutting sword because they were better for thrusting through the gaps between the plates. The mace was also popular, as was the lance. Other weapons, such as the short axe, could be used on horseback, while long-handled staff weapons, held in both hands, could be used on foot.

At the ready
The double-edged cutting sword, shown in this 13th-century effigy, could tear mail links apart.

The couched lance
Early 14th-century knights charge with lances "couched" under their arms.

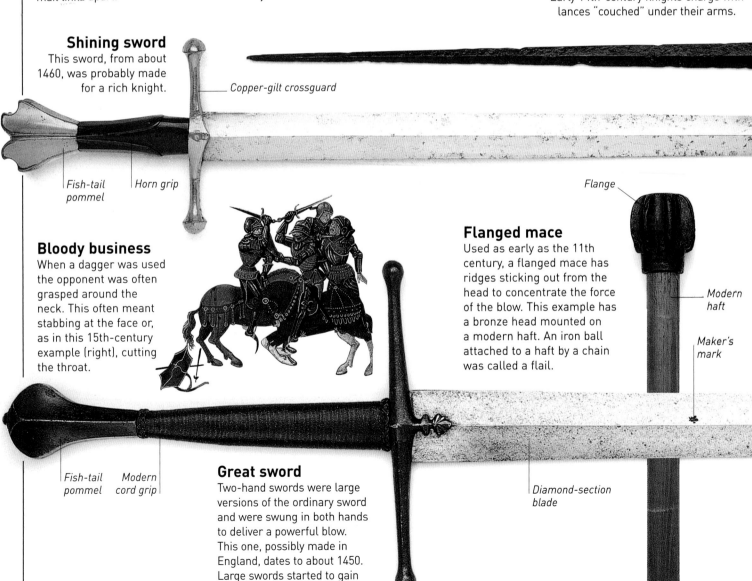

Shining sword
This sword, from about 1460, was probably made for a rich knight.

Copper-gilt crossguard

Fish-tail pommel *Horn grip*

Bloody business
When a dagger was used the opponent was often grasped around the neck. This often meant stabbing at the face or, as in this 15th-century example (right), cutting the throat.

Flanged mace
Used as early as the 11th century, a flanged mace has ridges sticking out from the head to concentrate the force of the blow. This example has a bronze head mounted on a modern haft. An iron ball attached to a haft by a chain was called a flail.

Flange

Modern haft

Maker's mark

Fish-tail pommel *Modern cord grip*

Great sword
Two-hand swords were large versions of the ordinary sword and were swung in both hands to deliver a powerful blow. This one, possibly made in England, dates to about 1450. Large swords started to gain popularity in the 13th century.

Diamond-section blade

Diamond-profile blade

Crossguard   *Modern cord grip*   *Wheel pommel with cap*

Getting the point
On this sharply pointed sword from the 14th century, the old-style blade with a central groove, or fuller, has been replaced by a stiffer one with a diamond-shaped profile. This acute point could burst apart the links of a piece of mail.

Death or glory
The impact of two riders colliding at up to 72 kph (45 mph) made the pointed lance a lethal weapon. In this 15th-century picture a knight's lance has punched through the opponent's armour. The figure on the left has a heavy-bladed cutting sword called a falchion.

Weapon of rank
This 15th-century sword has a hollow in the pommel that would have born the owner's coat-of-arms.

Fig-shaped pommel

Hollow for small shield

Cutting a path
This 14th-century illustration shows pointed swords with sharp edges that could cause terrible injuries and cuts to the bones.

Short axe
Knights sometimes wielded two-handed axes, but the smaller, single-handed variety was easier to use on horseback. This 14th-century example, mounted on a modern haft, has the remains of long iron langets that ran down the haft to stop the axehead being cut off.

Part of langet

Single-edged blade

Remains of gilt decoration   *Rondel*

Dagger
Knights did not use daggers much until the 14th century. This is a late 15th-century rondel dagger, so called because of the protective iron discs at either end of the grip.

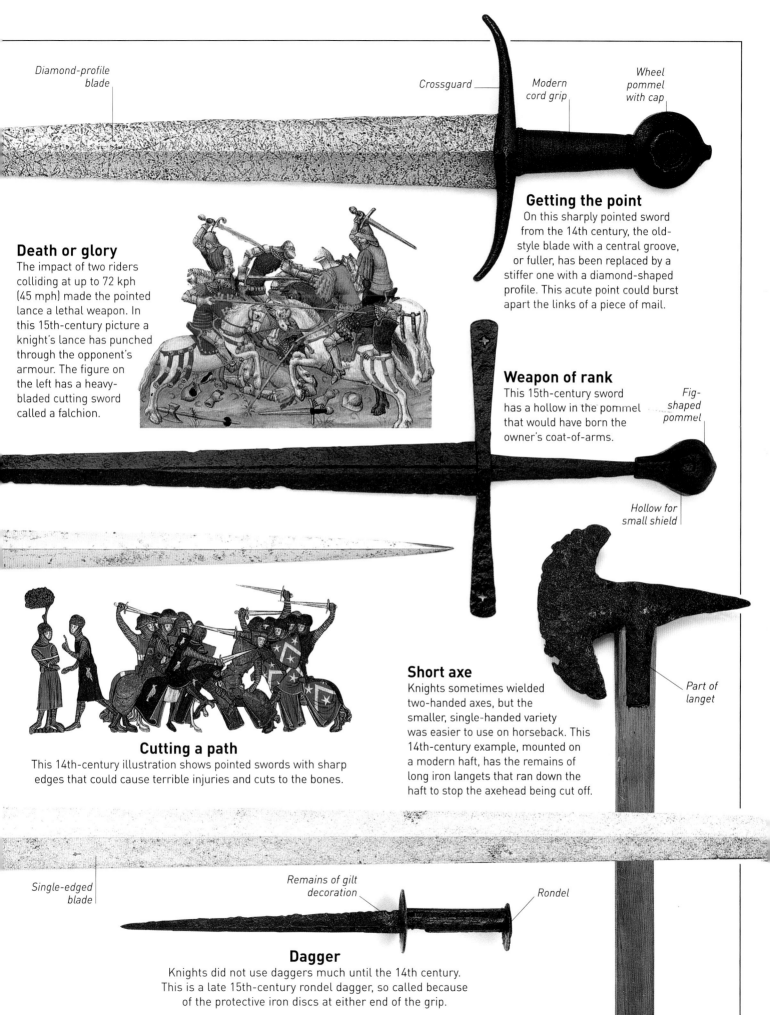

On horseback

Knights needed horses for warfare, hunting, jousting, travelling, and transporting baggage. The most costly animal was the destrier, or warhorse, which was tough and fast. Knights prized warhorses from Italy, France, and Spain. By the 13th century, knights usually had at least two warhorses: the courser was a swift hunting horse, though this name was sometimes applied to the warhorse, with destrier used for the jousting horse instead. For travelling, knights often used a palfrey, and packhorses called sumpter horses were used to carry baggage.

Fit for a king
An early 14th-century miniature shows the king of England on his warhorse. The richly decorated covering, or trapper, could be used to display heraldic arms.

Great horse
A destrier, or "Great Horse", wears armour on its head, neck, and chest. The knight in this 15th-century picture wears long spurs and shows the straight-legged riding position.

Etched and gilt decoration

"Eye" for leathers

Separately moving metal plates

Miniature goad
A knight wore spurs on his feet. He used them to urge on his horse. This 12th- or 13th-century prick spur is made of tinned iron.

Prick or goad

Rowel

Tread

Rowel spur
Rotating spurs with a spiked rowel replaced prick spurs by the early 14th century. This one dates to the second half of the 15th century.

Firm seat
Iron stirrups like this from the 14th century were worn with long straps so the knight was almost standing in them. This, together with high saddle boards, created a secure seat from which to fight.

Fine head

Horse armour was expensive and uncommon. If a knight could only afford one part, he would usually choose the shaffron, the piece for the head. This one, complete with crinet to protect the neck, is northern Italian and dates from about 1570.

Spike with spiral pattern

Brass plume-holder

Swift horse

A 15th-century woodcut shows a messenger on his mount. The horse is fast and has enough strength for a long trip.

Flanged eye-guard

Nose-guard

Jouster

Destrier – from the Latin *dextra*, meaning right – may suggest that the horse led with its right leg, so that if it swerved it would move away from an opponent.

Chain goes under horse's throat

Decorated metal boss

Poll plate

From the horse's mouth

Curb bits like this (left) created leverage from the long arms, which put pressure on the horse's mouth and gave very good control.

Muzzle

The German inscription at the top of this decorated steel frame reads: "As God wills, so is my aim." Below is a crowned Imperial eagle and the date 1561.

Ring for rein

Shaffron

This German shaffron (right) from the 1460s has a poll plate, attached by a brass hinge, to protect the top of the horse's head.

The castle

A castle could be a lord's home, his business headquarters, and a base for his soldiers. The first castles probably appeared in northwestern France in the ninth century, because of civil wars and Viking attacks. Although some early castles were built of stone, many consisted of earthworks and timber walls. In time knights began to use stone, then brick, as it was stronger and more fire-resistant.

Narrow slit
Windows near the ground were made small to guard against enemy missiles or soldiers climbing through. These narrow windows splayed on the inside, though, to let in light.

Motte and bailey
From the 11th century, many castles were given a mound called a motte – a last line of defence with a wooden tower on top. The courtyard, or bailey below it, held all the domestic buildings.

Strength in stone
The stone keep became common in the 11th and 12th centuries. By now, the bailey was often surrounded by stone walls with square towers. Round towers appeared in the 12th century.

Men at work
Stone castles cost a fortune to build and could take years to complete. The lord and the master mason chose a strong site and plan. Stone had to be brought in specially, and lime, sand, and water were needed for the mortar. The lord normally provided the materials and workforce.

Walls of defence
Concentric castles were first built in the 13th century. The inner wall was often higher so archers had a clear shot. Some old castles with keeps had outer walls added later, which gave another line of defence. Sometimes rivers were used to give broad water defences.

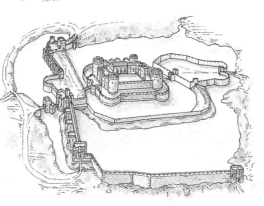

Cracking castle
Occasionally a stone tower was built on a motte, but the artificial mound was not always strong enough to take the weight. The 13th-century Clifford's Tower in York, England, has cracked as a result.

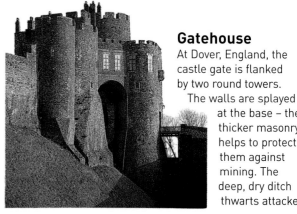

Gatehouse
At Dover, England, the castle gate is flanked by two round towers. The walls are splayed at the base – the thicker masonry helps to protect them against mining. The deep, dry ditch thwarts attackers.

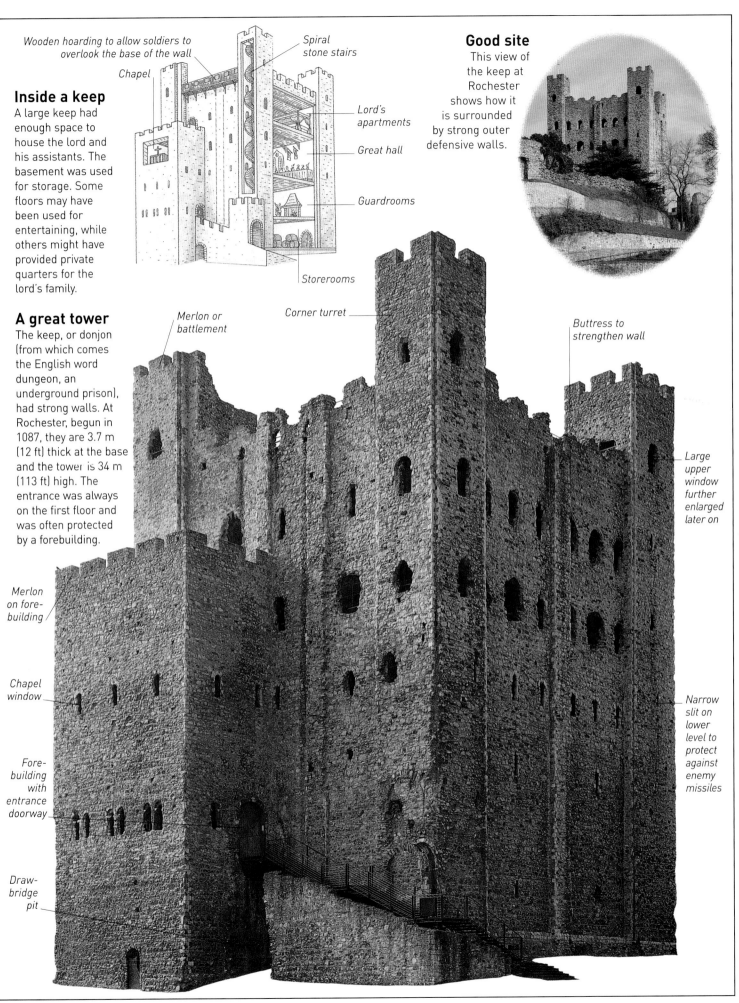

Wooden hoarding to allow soldiers to overlook the base of the wall

Spiral stone stairs

Chapel

Inside a keep
A large keep had enough space to house the lord and his assistants. The basement was used for storage. Some floors may have been used for entertaining, while others might have provided private quarters for the lord's family.

Lord's apartments

Great hall

Guardrooms

Storerooms

Good site
This view of the keep at Rochester shows how it is surrounded by strong outer defensive walls.

A great tower
The keep, or donjon (from which comes the English word dungeon, an underground prison), had strong walls. At Rochester, begun in 1087, they are 3.7 m (12 ft) thick at the base and the tower is 34 m (113 ft) high. The entrance was always on the first floor and was often protected by a forebuilding.

Merlon or battlement

Corner turret

Buttress to strengthen wall

Large upper window further enlarged later on

Merlon on forebuilding

Chapel window

Forebuilding with entrance doorway

Narrow slit on lower level to protect against enemy missiles

Drawbridge pit

The castle at war

Iron-clad wooden portcullis

Wooden doors barred from behind

The first obstacle for the enemy was a ditch all the way around the castle, which was sometimes filled with stakes. Moats – ditches that were often filled with water – were less common: they put off attackers from burrowing under the walls. Towers jutted out from the walls so that archers could shoot along the walls to repel any attackers. Small gates allowed the defenders to rush out and surprise the enemy.

Gatehouse
The gatehouse was always strongly defended. Usually a wooden lifting bridge spanned the ditch and a gate called a portcullis could form a barrier.

Vaulted ceiling
There are holes built into the gatehouse's ceiling. These allowed people to pour water down to put out fires or to drop boiling water or stones on attackers.

High turrets gave distinct views of approaching enemies

Gap, or crenel, through which defenders shoot

Merlon to protect defenders against missiles

Round flanking tower; the shape leaves no corners for a ram or miners

Machicolations along gate tower

Battlement on section of wall

Moat

Over the walls

This 14th-century picture shows the 11th-century crusader, Godfrey of Bouillon, attacking fortifications. His men are using scaling ladders.

Embrasure

An embrasure was an alcove in the wall with a narrow opening, or "loophole", to the outside. This allowed defenders to look and shoot out without showing themselves.

Flanking towers

This picture was taken looking up the front of the castle. Flanking towers jut out on either side to protect the gate. The battlements are thrust forwards so that they overhang the walls. Water could be poured through the holes to put out fires or to repel enemies.

Stone corbel supports the battlement

At siege

The attackers and defenders are using siege engines (pp. 26–27) to hurl missiles.

Knightly stronghold

Bodiam Castle in Sussex, England, was built in 1385 by Sir Edward Dalyngrigge amid fears of a French invasion. It has a single stone curtain wall with round towers at the corners and is surrounded by a moat to protect the occupants.

Turret, or watchtower

Lancet window to let in light but keep out missiles

Siege warfare

An enemy attacking a castle would make a formal demand for the people inside to surrender. If this was rejected, they would try to take the castle by siege. There were two methods. The first was to surround the castle and prevent anyone leaving or going in, thereby starving the defenders into submission. The second was to use force, including catapults or battering rams to break down the walls.

Counterpoise arm

Sling

Weighted box

Sling pouch

Rope to pull arm down again

Trebuchet
The trebuchet was first used in Europe in the 12th century. It worked on the principle of counterpoise – there was a pivoting wooden arm with a heavy weight at one end and a sling, containing a missile such as a stone, at the other. As the weight dropped down, the sling flew up, launching the missile toward the castle.

Hauling rope

Pulling your weight
The traction trebuchet worked like the counterpoise version, except the arm was moved by a team of men hauling on ropes. This meant that the machine was smaller than the counterpoise type and could not throw such large stones, but it could be reloaded more quickly.

Assault
Enemies attack a fortress with scaling ladders while crossbowmen and handgunners cover the assault. The attackers are also using a cannon to blast holes in the stonework.

Old and new
A trebuchet towers over a gunner and his cannon in this 15th-century picture.

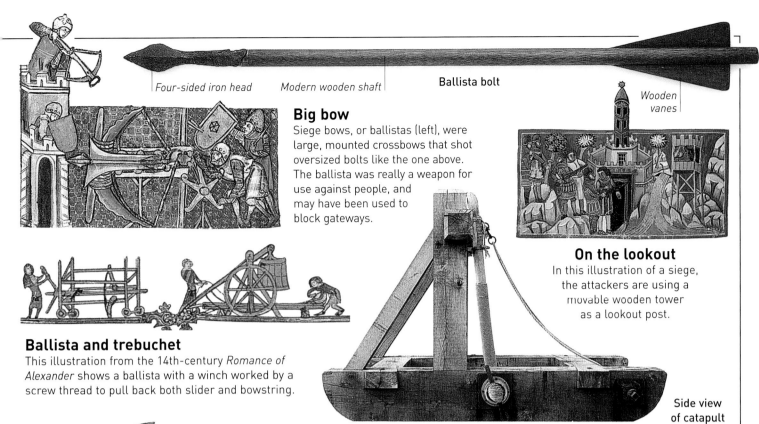

Four-sided iron head   Modern wooden shaft   Ballista bolt   Wooden vanes

Big bow
Siege bows, or ballistas (left), were large, mounted crossbows that shot oversized bolts like the one above. The ballista was really a weapon for use against people, and may have been used to block gateways.

On the lookout
In this illustration of a siege, the attackers are using a movable wooden tower as a lookout post.

Ballista and trebuchet
This illustration from the 14th-century *Romance of Alexander* shows a ballista with a winch worked by a screw thread to pull back both slider and bowstring.

Side view of catapult

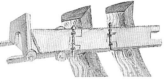

In theory
This is a design for a wooden bridge and covered penthouse to enable attackers to cross a ditch safely. It comes from a manuscript full of ingenious military ideas.

Wooden cup for missile

Throwing arm

Rope to winch arm down

Skein of twisted ropes provides power

Catapult in use

Surrender
This 15th-century illustration shows the defenders formally surrendering. If taken after a siege, a town or castle was occasionally looted by the soldiers as its occupants had refused to give up on request.

Front view of catapult

Pulling power
This catapult used the pulling power of a skein of twisted ropes, sinews, or even hair, to force the arm up against a bar. When winched back and released, the arm flew up, launching its missile from a wooden cup.

Armed to fight

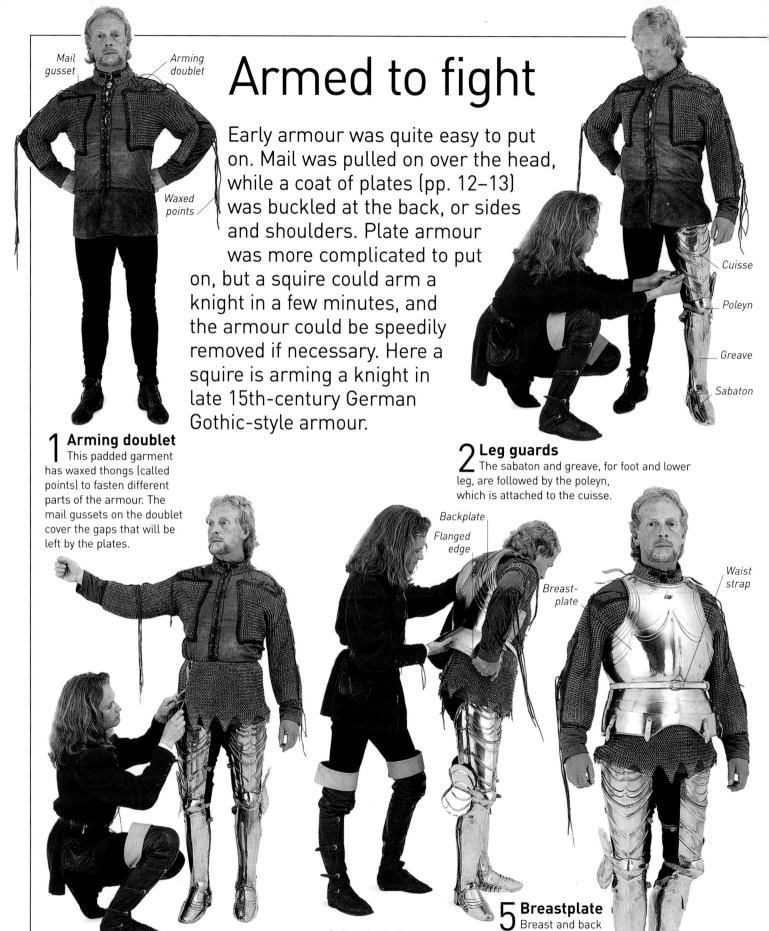

Mail gusset

Arming doublet

Waxed points

Early armour was quite easy to put on. Mail was pulled on over the head, while a coat of plates (pp. 12–13) was buckled at the back, or sides and shoulders. Plate armour was more complicated to put on, but a squire could arm a knight in a few minutes, and the armour could be speedily removed if necessary. Here a squire is arming a knight in late 15th-century German Gothic-style armour.

Cuisse

Poleyn

Greave

Sabaton

1 Arming doublet
This padded garment has waxed thongs (called points) to fasten different parts of the armour. The mail gussets on the doublet cover the gaps that will be left by the plates.

2 Leg guards
The sabaton and greave, for foot and lower leg, are followed by the poleyn, which is attached to the cuisse.

Backplate

Flanged edge

Breast-plate

Waist strap

3 Mail skirt
Mail around the waist protects the groin, which is not fully covered by the plates. Using flexible mail here makes it easier to bend or sit.

4 Backplate
The backplate is offered up into position. It has a flanged lower edge to deflect weapons from the buttocks and legs.

5 Breastplate
Breast and back together are called the cuirass. They are secured by the waist straps and are joined at the shoulders.

Pauldron

Besagew

Vambrace

Vambrace

Couter

7 Gauntlets, sword, and dagger

The gauntlets are fitted with a leather glove so the knight can grip his weapons. His sword belt has straps to hold the scabbard at a convenient angle. A rondel dagger hangs at his right side.

Leather glove inside gauntlet

Rondel dagger

Sword belt

Sword

6 Protecting the arms

The upper arm guard (vambrace) and elbow piece (couter) are tied by laces. The pauldron and besagew protect the shoulder and armpit.

Arming a knight

A rare picture from about 1450 shows a knight being armed for foot combat.

10 Fully armed

The knight holds a mace. Armed from head to foot (or cap-a-pie), he is now ready to mount his warhorse.

Bevor

Helmet

Mace

8 Bevor

A chin defence, or bevor, is added to protect the lower half of the face when wearing the sallet, a helmet especially popular in Germany.

Rowel spur

9 Spurs and helmet

The knight's rowel spurs (pp. 20–21) are buckled to his feet. The helmet, lined inside for comfort and to cushion blows, is placed on his head. It has a chin strap.

The enemy

Knights soon found themselves facing dangerous enemies. The English axemen at Hastings in 1066 cut down Norman knights, while Scottish spear formations stopped cavalry charges at Bannockburn in 1314, a strategy also favoured by the Swiss, who used pikes. Different types of bow were highly effective against mounted knights. In early 15th-century Bohemia (now part of the Czech Republic) the Hussites blasted German knights, using the first massed guns.

The longbow

This type of bow was usually made of a stave of yew wood about the height of the archer. It was usually fitted with horn nocks at the tips to take the hemp string. War bows probably needed a pull of at least 36 kg (80 lb), and many may have been far more powerful.

Barbed arrow-head

Leather bracer

Stave of yew wood

Horn nock to take string

Arrows stood in front for quick reloading

Slinger

Some infantrymen used slings. The stone or lead bullets were lethal if they struck a man in the face, but they could not damage armour. Sometimes a sling was attached to a wooden handle to increase range.

A bristling hedge

Cavalrymen were unhappy about forcing their horses against spears or pikes, as infantry in close formation with a "hedge" of these weapons could hold off mounted knights.

An archer

Longbows were used in many European countries, although on the mainland the crossbow was much more popular. When drawing a longbow, the string was brought back somewhere between the cheek and the ear. The leather bracer protected the arms from an accidental slap from the string; a leather tab protected the drawer's fingers. Archers wore various pieces of defensive armour, or just a simple padded doublet, as shown here.

At the butts
Archers needed constant practice to maintain their skills. In this 14th-century picture, English archers shoot at the butts – targets set up on earthen mounds.

The goose feather
Nock inset into shaft *Goose feather* *Binding*

Fletchings, or feather flights, make the arrow spin for a truer flight. Usually goose feathers were used for the the arrows. The shaft was commonly made from ash wood.

Fragment of shaft

General-purpose

Bodkin   Bodkin

General-purpose   Broadhead

Arrowheads
Depending on their use, arrowheads had various shapes. Broadheads were barbed for use against animals, while bodkins were for penetrating armour. There were also general-purpose arrowheads.

Long-range fighting
Arrows from a longbow could probably reach a distance of about 300 m (984 ft), so could be dropped on an advancing enemy. This was done by shooting the arrows upwards. Bodkins could punch through mail links at extreme range, and cavalry horses were also vulnerable.

Bodkin

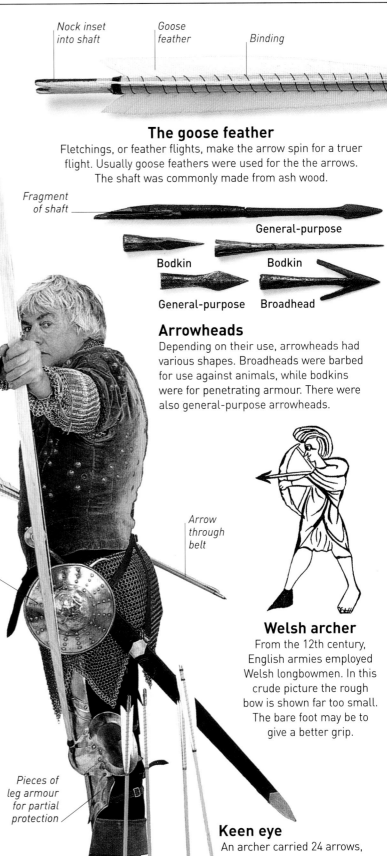

Steel buckler or fist shield

Arrow through belt

Pieces of leg armour for partial protection

Welsh archer
From the 12th century, English armies employed Welsh longbowmen. In this crude picture the rough bow is shown far too small. The bare foot may be to give a better grip.

Keen eye
An archer carried 24 arrows, known as a sheaf, and when these were shot more were brought from supply wagons. They would often stick their arrows into the ground in front of them, so they were ready to be shot quickly.

Longbow versus crossbow
A skilled archer (such as the men in the centre of this 15th-century illustration) might release 12 arrows per minute. A crossbowman (on the left) could only shoot two bolts in the same time, but these would penetrate deeply.

Into battle

The rules of chivalry dictated that knights should show courtesy to defeated enemies, but this code was not always observed. Knights often showed little mercy to foot soldiers, cutting them down ruthlessly in pursuit. Much was at stake in a battle – defeat might mean the loss of an army or even a throne. So commanders preferred to raid enemy territory, as this brought extra supplies as well as destroying property.

Warrior kings
Many medieval kings were shown on their great seal as head of their army, on horseback and wearing full armour. Here Henry I, King of England (1100–1135) and Duke of Normandy, wears a mail coat and conical helmet.

Fighting on foot
Although knights were trained as horsemen, on many occasions it was thought better for a large part of an army to dismount and form a solid body, often supported by archers and groups of cavalry. In this 14th-century illustration, dismounted English and French knights and men-at-arms clash on a bridge. Archers and crossbowmen assist them.

Caltrops
Only a few centimetres high, iron-made caltrops were scattered over the battleground to lame horses or men from the opposing army who accidentally trod on them. When thrown, they always landed with one spike pointing upward.

In pursuit
A 13th-century battle scene (above) shows one force pursuing the opposing side. Often the pursuers did not hesitate to strike at men with their backs turned. However, breaking ranks to chase the enemy could sometimes put the rest of your army in danger.

Wall of horses

Armour of the 12th century was similar in many parts of Europe, but fighting methods could vary. Rather than using lances to stab or throw, the Italian knights on this stone carving are tucking them under their arms. Each side charges in close formation, hoping to steamroller over their opponents.

Shock of battle

This 15th-century picture shows the crash of two opposing cavalry forces in full plate armour. Those struck down by lances in the first line, even if only slightly wounded, were liable to be trampled by the horses of either the enemy or of their own knights following behind.

Spoils of war

When an army was defeated the victors would often capture the baggage, which could contain many valuables, especially if the ousted leader was a prince. In this 14th-century Italian picture, the victors are examining the spoils.

Shock waves

This 16th-century German woodcut shows mounted knights galloping towards the enemy. The first line has made contact while those behind follow with lances still raised.

One spike always points upwards

Three spikes rest on the ground

Castle life

The castle did not just house a garrison, it was home for the knight and his household. Everyone had their meals in the great hall; day-to-day business was also done here. There was also a kitchen (often a separate building in case of fire), a chapel, an armourer's workshop, a smithy, stables, kennels, pens for animals, a water supply – like a well – and large storerooms to keep the castle well stocked. Castles were also useful resting places for nobles when they were travelling.

Coat-of-arms

Song and dance
Music often accompanied meals. Dances usually involved many people who held hands in various types of ring dance.

Wall sconce
This gilt-copper 16th-century wall sconce for burning candles bears the Castelnau-LaLoubere family's coat-of-arms, encircled by the collar of the Order of St Michael.

Silver cruet
This 14th-century silver vessel was kept in a chapel to hold the holy water or wine used at Mass.

At the lord's table
On this 1316 manuscript, Lancelot tells King Arthur and the whole household gathered in the great hall of his adventures.

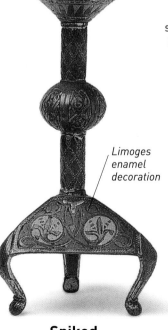
Limoges enamel decoration

Spiked
This chapel candlestick, dating to about 1230, had a long spike to take the candle.

A game of chess
Duke Francis of Angoulême (later king of France) plays chess with his wife Marguerite in a picture from around 1504. Being a wargame, chess was popular with knights.

Blazing fire
Large fireplaces could be set in the thick stone walls of castles.

Hand basin

Pairs of basins like this, called gemellions, were used to wash peoples' hands at the table. A servant would pour water over the person's hands from one basin into the other, then dry the hands with a towel.

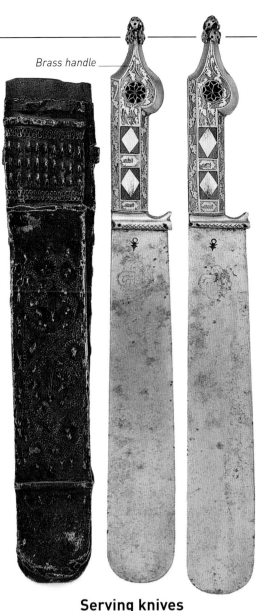

Brass handle

A knight kneels before his lady

Houschold musician

Serving knives

Pairs of broad-bladed knives, like these 15th-century German ones, were used for serving food. The leather sheath has lost its cap.

Chamber pot

Although richer people might use chamber pots like this, castles often had lavatories built into the walls. A chute sent human waste beyond the castle wall.

Play the game

Board games like draughts – shown in this 14th-century depiction – and backgammon were popular.

Steelyard weight

Bronze weights

This 13th-century steelyard weight was hung from a pivoting metal arm to work out the weight of an object placed on the other end.

Royal arms

Manor lords

Some knights were mercenary soldiers who fought for money. Others, particularly until the 13th century, lived at their lord's expense as household troops in his castle, or were given pieces of land by their lord. Such a man became lord of the manor and lived off its produce. He lived in a manor house, often of stone and with its own defences. He held a large part of the manor and "his" peasants – workers of varying status – owed him service in return for their homes.

Home defence
Stokesay is a fortified manor house in Shropshire, England. Built mostly in the 13th century, it consists of a hall and chamber block with a tower at each end.

Original die

My seal on it
Noblemen were often illiterate, so they used a wax seal to sign documents. This is Robert FitzWalter's seal; he made King John sign the Magna Carta in 1215.

Modern cast

Name of Robert FitzWalter, owner of the seal

All in the game
This wealthy 14th-century Italian couple play a board game. Usually, musicans or poets entertained knights.

Ivory chess pieces
These 12th-century Scandinavian chessmen are carved from walrus ivory.

Queen

King

Bishop

Knight

Warder (Rook)

Uphill struggle
Medieval peasants grew and harvested crops. This 14th-century picture shows peasants coaxing a hay cart up a steep slope.

Garden of delight
In this 15th-century manor, one house is made of timber filled in with wattle and daub (mud or clay). Close by is an orchard of fruit trees.

Like father, like son
These details from a 15th-century altar show a praying knight with his sons. The eldest son would become a knight; his daughters would hope to marry noblemen. Younger children often went into the church.

Decorated casket
This large casket belonged to a wealthy 15th-century family. It is made of wood covered in bone panels carved with biblical scenes.

The lord
The status and rank of a lord varied. Some lords were powerful men who held a number of manors. A bailiff would look after the running of the estates when the lord was away. He might visit a town to meet trade merchants or to borrow money from money-lenders.

Manor ladies

The life of the lady
The lady ruled the kitchens and living quarters. She had officials to run the household affairs, but she checked all the accounts and agreed to any expenses. She also received guests and arranged for their accommodation. Ladies-in-waiting were her friends, maidservants attended her, and nurses looked after her children.

In the Middle Ages, women, even those of noble rank, had fewer rights than women today. Many women had an arranged marriage by the age of 14. But the lady was her husband's equal in private life. She could support her husband and take responsibility for the castle when he was away. She might even have to defend the castle in her husband's absence if it was besieged and hold it against her enemies.

Dalliance
This illustration from the medieval poem *The Romance of the Rose* shows courtly love. Here, women listen to a song near a fountain. However, in reality many women would not have had time for this.

The white swan
This 15th-century brooch is known as the Dunstable Swan. The swan was used as a badge by the House of Lancaster (one of the English royal families), particularly by the Princes of Wales, heirs to the throne.

Bad news
A lady swoons on hearing of her husband's death. Marriages were arranged by the couples' families, but a husband and wife could grow to love one another.

Women of accomplishment
Some women could read and write, and speak foreign languages. In this picture, ladies with books represent Philosophy and the Liberal Arts.

Jewels
Women liked to display their rank with rings and brooches. The 15th-century brooch at the top is probably Flemish and depicts a female; the 14th-century English brooch is decorated with coiled monsters.

On bended knees
A knight places his hands in those of his lady. He is indicating that he will be her servant – an ideal of courtly love that was not borne out in practice.

English gold brooch

"Suitable" jobs
Some men thought teaching women to read was dangerous. In this 15th-century picture, one woman spins woollen thread while another combs out the wool.

Pommel

Cantle

Sidesaddle
Noblewomen were often active hunters. This medallion from 1477 shows Mary of Burgundy carrying her hawk on her wrist and riding sidesaddle, a method that solved the difficulty of sitting on a horse in a long dress.

Tale on a saddle
This 15th-century German saddle is made of wood covered with plaques of staghorn, on which are carved the figure of a man and a woman. They speak of their love and the woman asks: "But if the war should end?"

Carved plaque

The ideal of chivalry

Although knights were men of war, they traditionally behaved in a civil way towards their enemies. In the 12th century, this kind of behaviour was extended to form a knightly code of conduct, emphasizing courtly manners towards women. Churchmen liked the idea of high standards and made the knighting ceremony (pp. 10–11) a religious occasion. Books on chivalry appeared, though in reality knights often found it difficult to live up to the ideal.

St George
According to legend, St George was a soldier martyred by the Romans in about 350 CE. During the Middle Ages, stories appeared telling how he rescued a king's daughter from a dragon. This carved ivory shows St George.

Knight in shining armour
This 15th-century shield shows a knight kneeling before his lady. The words on the scroll mean "You or death".

True-love knots
Medallions like this were sometimes made to mark special occasions, such as marriages. This one was struck to commemorate the marriage of Margaret of Austria to the Duke of Savoy in 1502. The knots are the badge of Savoy.

What's in a name?
This 15th-century book *The Lovelorn Heart* illustrates how people in medieval romance often stood for objects or feelings. Here the knight, called Cueur (meaning Heart), reads an inscription while his companion, Desire, lies sleeping.

Sir Lancelot and Guinevere

King Arthur was probably a fifth-century warrior, but the legends of the king and the knights of the round table gained popularity in 13th-century Europe. They tell of the love between Arthur's queen, Guinevere, and Sir Lancelot. Here, Sir Lancelot crosses a bridge to rescue Guinevere.

Royal champion

Sir Edward Dymoke was the champion of Queen Elizabeth I of England. At her coronation banquet, it was his job to ride fully armed into the hall and hurl his gauntlet to the ground to defy anyone who wished to question the queen's right to rule. This challenge was made at every coronation until that of George IV in 1821.

The knight of the cart

The brave Sir Lancelot's love affair with Queen Guinevere brought him shame. This illustration shows Lancelot meeting a dwarf who offers to tell him where Guinevere is if he will ride in the cart. It was thought a disgrace for a knight to travel in a cart, as they were usually on horseback.

Lock

Corner reinforcement

Tragic lovers

This 12th-century box tells the tale of the knight Tristan, who accidentally drank a love potion and fell in love with Iseult, the bride of his uncle, King Mark.

The tournament

Fighting men have always trained for battle. Tournaments probably started in the 11th century as practice for war in which two teams of knights fought a mock battle, called a tourney or mêlée. Defeated knights gave up their horse and armour to the victor. Other contests, such as jousts (pp. 44–45), also appeared. In the 17th century, the tournament was replaced in most countries by displays of horsemanship, called carousels.

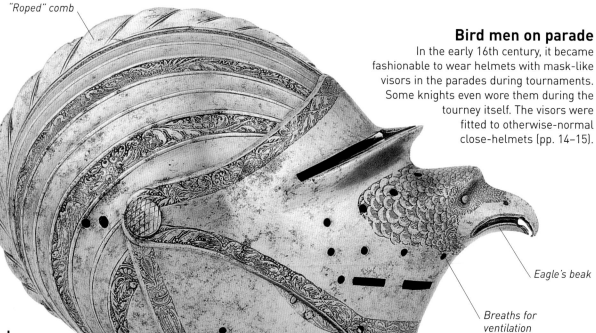

"Roped" comb

Bird men on parade
In the early 16th century, it became fashionable to wear helmets with mask-like visors in the parades during tournaments. Some knights even wore them during the tourney itself. The visors were fitted to otherwise-normal close-helmets (pp. 14–15).

Eagle's beak

Breaths for ventilation

Flying banners
The colourful array of banners at a tournament display coats-of-arms and other kinds of fanciful designs. The knights also wore large crests on their helms, even when these were no longer worn in battle.

Devil

Devil take you
The church disliked tournaments because so much blood was often spilt. This 14th-century picture shows a devil waiting to seize the souls of knights killed in a tourney.

A knight disgraced
The women viewed the banners and helms of the contestants before the tourney. If a lady knew that a knight had done wrong, his helm was taken down and he was banned.

Club tourney

In this type of tourney, two teams use blunt swords and clubs. Their crested helmets are fitted with protective face grilles. Each knight has a banner-bearer, while attendants (called varlets) stand ready in case he falls. The knight of honour rides between two ropes that separate the teams; ladies and judges are in the stands. Although the tournament grounds, or lists, had become smaller, the artist of this illustration has squashed them up to fit everything in.

Hole to take lance

Etched and gilt decoration

Vamplate

Vamplate and locking-gauntlet

The vamplate was fixed over the lance to guard the knight's hand. Once the knight had gripped his sword, the locking-gauntlet was locked shut so the sword was not lost in combat.

Locking-gauntlet

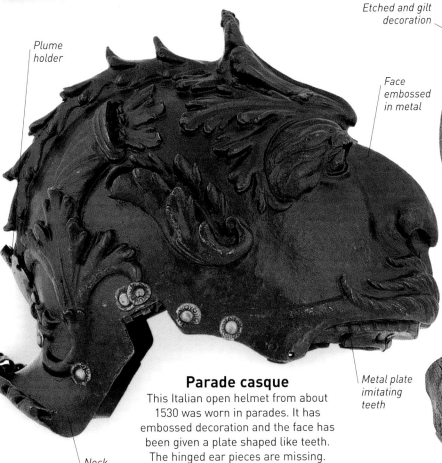

Plume holder

Face embossed in metal

Parade casque

This Italian open helmet from about 1530 was worn in parades. It has embossed decoration and the face has been given a plate shaped like teeth. The hinged ear pieces are missing.

Metal plate imitating teeth

Neck guard

The joust

During the 13th century, jousts were added to tournaments. In this exciting contest, two knights would charge towards one another at top speed and try to knock each other of their horse with a single blow off their lance. A knight could also score points if he broke an opponent's lance or shield. Sometimes, a sharp, deadly lances were used – these were called "jousts of war". Some knights preferred to use a lance fitted with a blunt tip – these were known as "jousts of peace".

Eye slit

Frog-mouthed helm
This 15th-century helmet was used for jousts of peace. The wearer could see his opponent by leaning forward during the charge. He straightened up at the moment of impact, so that the "frog-mouthed" lower lip protected his eyes from the lance-head.

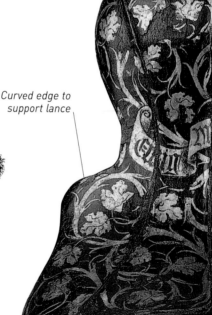

Curved edge to support lance

Lancer's shield
This 15th-century wooden shield covered in leather was probably used for the Rennen. The lance could be placed in the recess in the side.

Germanic jousters
Knights in Germany practised the "Rennen", a version of the jousts of war. No barrier was used, so the knights' legs were partially protected by metal shields.

Wooden lances
By the 16th century, wooden lances were made to splinter easily. Slightly thinner than those used for jousting, this 17th-century lance (left) was used to spear a ring hanging from a bracket.

Parade before the tilt
Knights paraded beside the tilt, or barrier, before the jousting commenced. Although this scene was painted in the 15th century, it depicts the jousts from 1390, before the tilt was introduced. Attendants with spare lances accompany the knights.

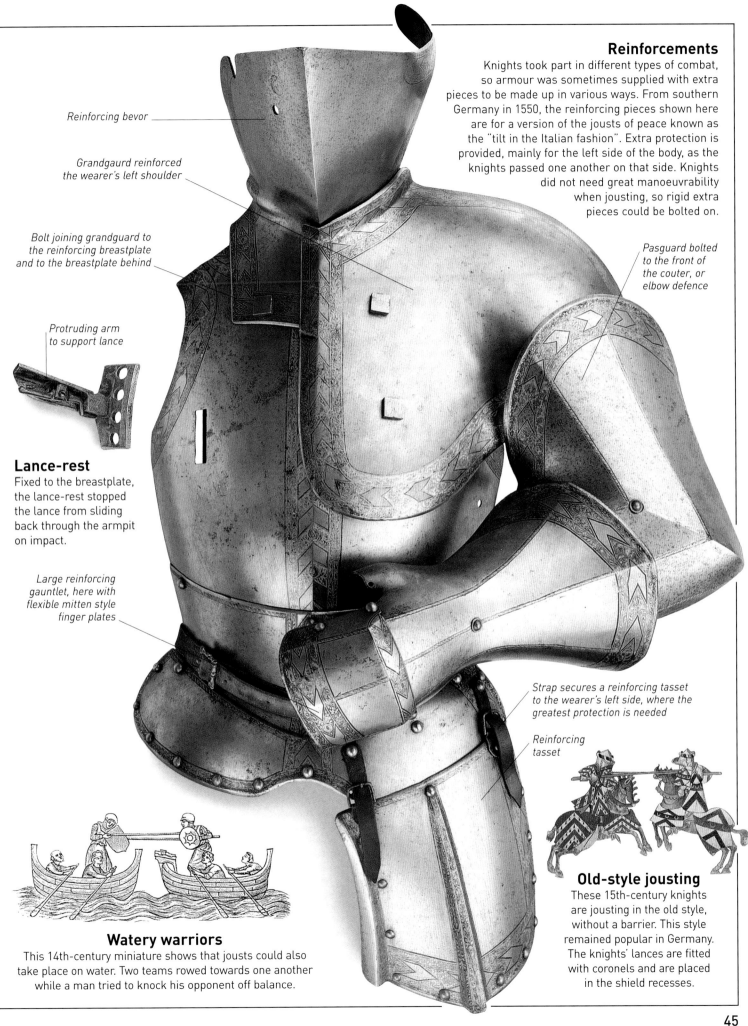

Reinforcing bevor

Grandgaurd reinforced
the wearer's left shoulder

Bolt joining grandguard to
the reinforcing breastplate
and to the breastplate behind

Protruding arm
to support lance

Lance-rest
Fixed to the breastplate,
the lance-rest stopped
the lance from sliding
back through the armpit
on impact.

Large reinforcing
gauntlet, here with
flexible mitten style
finger plates

Reinforcements
Knights took part in different types of combat,
so armour was sometimes supplied with extra
pieces to be made up in various ways. From southern
Germany in 1550, the reinforcing pieces shown here
are for a version of the jousts of peace known as
the "tilt in the Italian fashion". Extra protection is
provided, mainly for the left side of the body, as the
knights passed one another on that side. Knights
did not need great manoeuvrability
when jousting, so rigid extra
pieces could be bolted on.

Pasguard bolted
to the front of
the couter, or
elbow defence

Strap secures a reinforcing tasset
to the wearer's left side, where the
greatest protection is needed

Reinforcing
tasset

Watery warriors
This 14th-century miniature shows that jousts could also
take place on water. Two teams rowed towards one another
while a man tried to knock his opponent off balance.

Old-style jousting
These 15th-century knights
are jousting in the old style,
without a barrier. This style
remained popular in Germany.
The knights' lances are fitted
with coronels and are placed
in the shield recesses.

Foot combat

In some 13th-century jousts, the knights dismounted and fought on with swords. By the 14th century, such foot combats were popular in their own right. Each knight was allowed a set number of blows, delivered alternately. From the 15th-century, each man sometimes threw a javelin before fighting with a sword, axe, or staff weapon. Later, such combats were replaced by foot tournaments in which two teams fought across a barrier.

At the ready
This detail from a 16th-century Flemish tapestry shows contestants waiting to take part in foot combat over the barrier.

Visor

Sword cuts

Formal fight
Foot combats in the 15th century took place without a barrier, so the contestants protected their legs with armour. The most common helmet for these contests was the great basinet (pp. 12–13).

Hand-threaded screw

Brow reinforce
This plate was screwed to the visor of the helmet shown on the right.

Chin piece

Holes for laces of cross-straps to secure the head

Close-helmet
This 1555 helmet for foot tournaments is so richly gilded that it is surprising that it was ever worn in actual combat. However, the sword cuts show that it must have been used.

Thick steel for extra safety

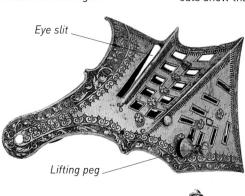

Visor hinge

Neck guard

Foot combat
Helmets, such as this 16th-century one (above), had to be able to withstand direct blows at close quarters, so the steel might be thicker than that used on a battle helmet.

Eye slit

Lifting peg

Exchange visor
Two threaded bolts allowed the visor to be removed from the helmet on the left and replaced with this one, which has a number of ventilation holes.

Trial by battle
Sometimes a charge of murder or treason was settled by foot combat. The contest went on until the accused was either killed or surrendered, in which case he was executed.

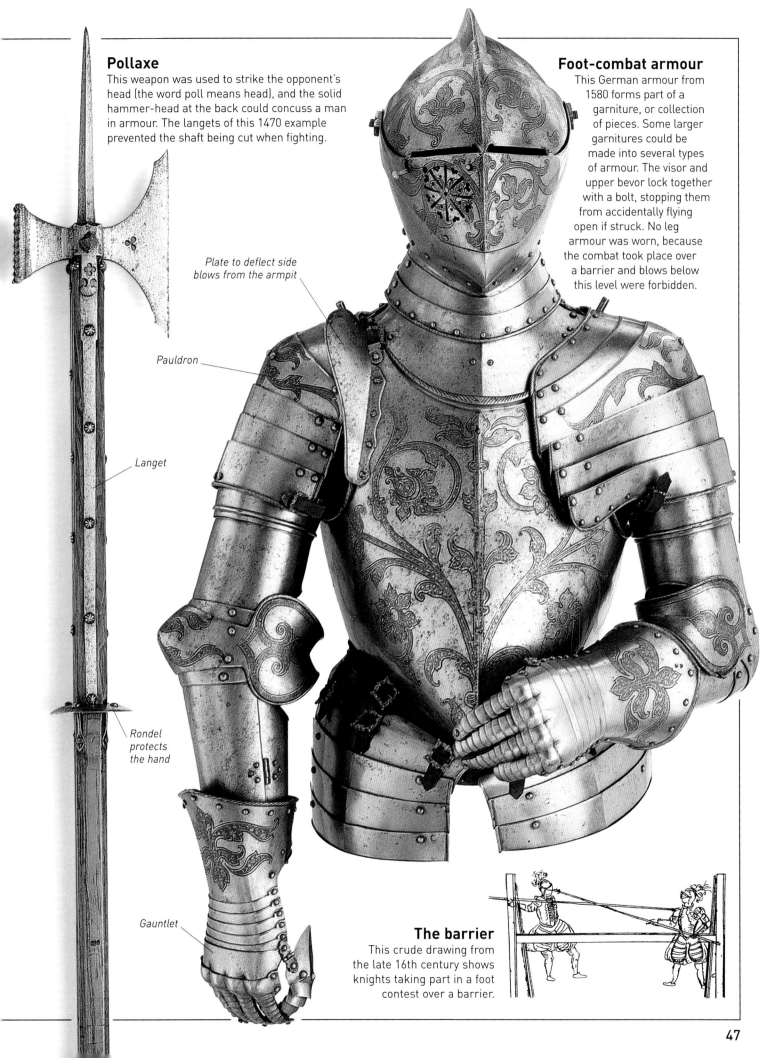

Pollaxe
This weapon was used to strike the opponent's head (the word poll means head), and the solid hammer-head at the back could concuss a man in armour. The langets of this 1470 example prevented the shaft being cut when fighting.

Foot-combat armour
This German armour from 1580 forms part of a garniture, or collection of pieces. Some larger garnitures could be made into several types of armour. The visor and upper bevor lock together with a bolt, stopping them from accidentally flying open if struck. No leg armour was worn, because the combat took place over a barrier and blows below this level were forbidden.

Plate to deflect side blows from the armpit

Pauldron

Langet

Rondel protects the hand

Gauntlet

The barrier
This crude drawing from the late 16th century shows knights taking part in a foot contest over a barrier.

Heraldry

In the 12th century, shield designs became more standardized in a system known as heraldry. This enabled a knight to be identified by symbols on his shield, or a full coat-of-arms. A knight carried one coat-of-arms, and this passed to his eldest son when he died. Other children used slightly different versions of their father's arms.

Or, a pale gules

Azure, a fess embattled or

Sable, a cross engrailed or

Lozengy argent and gules

Vert, a crescent or

Azure, a fleur-de-lys or

Gules, a spur argent

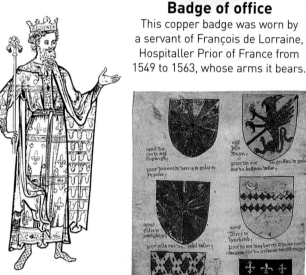

Badge of office
This copper badge was worn by a servant of François de Lorraine, Hospitaller Prior of France from 1549 to 1563, whose arms it bears.

Costume design
The fleur-de-lys, heraldic emblem of France, is used to decorate this tunic, although true heraldry forbids gold placed on white or silver.

Roll of arms
The Carlisle Roll contains 277 shields of King Edward III's personnel on his visit to Carlisle, England, in 1334.

Heraldic jar
Coats-of-arms were also placed on objects. This jar, from about 1500, has quartered arms, in which the arms of two families joined by marriage appear twice together.

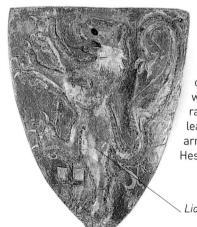

A knight's shield
This rare surviving shield from the 13th century is made from wood, which has a lion rampant moulded in leather. These are the arms of a ruler of Hesse, Germany.

Lion rampant

Arms of Cosimo de' Medici

Colourful spectacle
In this 15th-century picture, knights' shields hang over the sides of boats, largely for display. Colourful heraldic banners bore the arms of their knightly owners. The French royal arms appear on trumpet banners.

Gules, a lion rampant or

Or, a lion sejant regardant purpure

Gules, a swan argent

Sword arms
Etched with the arms of Cosimo de' Medici, Duke of Florence, this Italian falchion, or short cutting sword, dates from the 16th century.

Pommel of gilt bronze cast in shape of a lion's head

Making an impression
The bezel of this large 14th-century gold signet ring is engraved with heraldic arms of the de Grailly family. Above are the letters: "EID Gre", probably meaning: "This is the seal of Jean de Grailly."

Azure, a dolphin naiant argent

Or, a dragon rampant vert

Coat-of-arms
This brass of Sir Thomas Blenerhasset (died 1531) shows the heraldic arms on his coat armour, the name given to the surcoat.

Spanish plate
The Spanish kingdom of Castile had a castle for its arms, while Leon used a lion. The two kingdoms united in 1230. The background design of this Spanish dish of about 1425 is influenced by Spanish Muslims.

Or, a portcullis purpure

Key to arms	
Or	Gold
Argent	Silver
Gules	Red
Azure	Blue
Sable	Black
Vert	Green
Purpure	Purple

Azure, a sun in splendour or

Hunting

Medieval monarchs and lords were fond of hunting. The sport provided fresh meat, as well as helping to train knights for war. The Norman kings set aside vast areas of woodland for hunting in England. The animals hunted included deer, rabbits, boar, and birds. Sometimes, beaters drove the prey towards the huntsmen, who lay in wait. Hawking was also very popular. One 15th-century manuscript gives a list of hawks, showing how only the higher members of society could fly the best birds.

Flying to a lure
A lure was a dummy bird that the falconer swung from a long cord. The falcon would pounce on the lure, so that the falconer could retrieve his bird.

Noble beasts
This detail of the carving on the side of this crossbow tiller shows a stag hunt. Only rich people were allowed to hunt stags.

Steel pin to engage rack for spanning bow

Wooden tiller veneered with polished stag horn carved in relief

Wooden flights

Wooden feathers
Rather than feathers, one of these crossbow bolts from about 1470 has wooden flights.

For deer hunters
The blade of a 1540 German hunting sword, below, is etched with scenes of a stag hunt. Such swords were carried when hunting and were also used for general protection.

Wolf hunt
Huntsmen used meat to lure wolves, who followed the scent. Look-outs in trees warned of the wolf's approach and mastiff dogs flushed it out. This hunt is from a 14th-century hunting book of Gaston Phoebus, Count of Foix, France.

Frederick II, the falconer
This German emperor was so keen on falconry that in the 13th century he wrote a book on it, from which this picture comes.

Deer being driven into nets

Dogs chasing the deer

Hunting horn

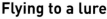

Man shooting squirrel

Falconer

On the hunt
A Flemish or German silver plaque of about 1600 shows hunting with hounds, falconry, and shooting. One hound catches a hare in front of three ladies, who watch with interest from their carriage.

Weapon at the ready
The crossbow was a popular hunting weapon. It could be used on horseback and easily reloaded. Because the bowstring was drawn back over the nut and held there until released by the trigger, the crossbow could be spanned ready in case any game was flushed out. Crossbows for use in hunting were sometimes lavishly decorated, as shown on this detailed 15th-century example.

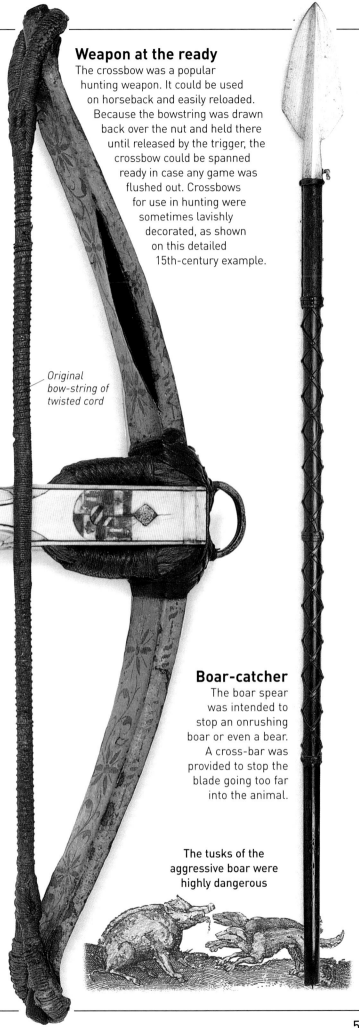

Original bow-string of twisted cord

Revolving nut released by trigger below

Triangular barbed head

Pet care
Hunting dogs needed to be looked after carefully and Gaston Phoebus recommended using herbal medicines to cure mange and diseases of the eye, ear, and throat. Broken legs were put in harnesses.

Boar-catcher
The boar spear was intended to stop an onrushing boar or even a bear. A cross-bar was provided to stop the blade going too far into the animal.

The tusks of the aggressive boar were highly dangerous

After them!
This 14th-century picture shows a lady blowing a hunting horn as she gallops after the dogs.

Faith and pilgrimage

The church played a major part in life in the Middle Ages. Western Europe was Roman Catholic until Protestantism took hold in some countries in the 16th century. Most people were religious and churches flourished, taking one-tenth of everyone's goods as a sort of tax. Some lords even became monks after a life of violence, hoping that this would make it easier for them to enter heaven.

Owner of the horn
This medallion shows Charles, Duke of Burgundy, who owned the Horn of St Hubert.

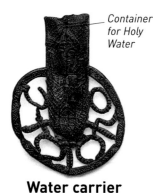

Container for Holy Water

Water carrier
People wore tiny containers, called ampullae, holding Holy Water to protect them from evil. This one has a picture of St Thomas Becket, killed at Canterbury, England, in 1170.

Lead pilgrim badge of St Catherine

Knight at prayer
The saints played a vital part in peoples' lives. This stained-glass window shows a knight praying at a statue of Mary Magdelene.

Symbols of faith
People often wore badges to show that they had been on a pilgrimage, such as this simple lead cross. Other symbols included Christ and the Virgin Mary, and the saints.

Lead seal showing the Virgin Mary holding the baby Jesus

Silver chalice
During mass, a chalice was used to hold the consecrated wine. This decorated one, which was made in Spain or Italy in the early 16th century, shows the wealth and importance of the Church. It is designed with six medallions that show Christ and some of the saints.

Head of saint

Horn of St Hubert

Medieval people liked to touch or even possess relics of the dead saints, even though some had no connection with the real saint. St Hubert was said to have seen the vision of a cross shining between a deer's antlers, and he became the patron saint of huntsmen.

Pelican in her piety

St John

Virgin Mary

To be a pilgrim

These 15th-century pilgrims are travelling to the Holy Land of Jerusalem, but getting there meant a long and dangerous journey. Pilgrims to Jerusalem wore a palm-leaf badge.

Crucified Christ

Missionary

The Church was always keen to convert others to Christianity, either through peaceful teaching or by more forceful methods. Here, Friar Oderic receives a blessing before he goes to the East as a missionary. Knights might also desire blessings before dangerous journeys.

St Nicholas

The Canterbury Tales

Around 1387, Geoffrey Chaucer (right) wrote *The Canterbury Tales*, which is about a pilgrimage. One tale sees a knight (left) and his son tell stories along the way to pass the time.

Chaucer's knight

Geoffrey Chaucer

Processional cross

This early 15th-century Italian silver cross has been partly gilded and decorated with enamels. The Virgin Mary, St John, and St Nicholas are shown on the arms of the cross. The pelican is a symbol of piety – people thought that she wounded herself in order to feed her young, a symbol of Christ bleeding for all sinners.

The crusades

In 1095 at Clermont, France, Pope Urban II launched a military expedition to take back the Christian holy places in Jerusalem from the Muslim Turks who ruled the Holy Land. This expedition became known as the First Crusade. Apart from a brief period in 1228–29 – when the German emperor Frederick II made an agreement with the Muslims – the crusaders failed in their quest. Even Richard the Lionheart, the warlike English king and a leader of the Third Crusade of 1190, knew that if he could capture Jerusalem, he would not be able to hold it. The crusades also preached against non-Catholic heretics in Europe.

People's crusade

In 1096, the French preacher Peter the Hermit led a mob from Cologne, Germany, towards Jerusalem. Though there were some knights in this People's Crusade, it was wiped out in Anatolia (modern Turkey) by the Turks.

Spanish crusaders

In Spain, from the 11th century, Christian armies fought the Muslims, or Moors, until their last stronghold fell in 1492. Warrior monks, such as the Order of Santiago seen here, helped the Christian reconquest of Spain.

Taking ship

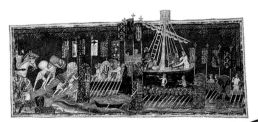

There were two routes from Europe to the Holy Land: the dangerous road overland or across the Mediterranean Sea. The Italian city-states of Venice, Pisa, and Genoa, eager for new trade, often provided ships.

The Mamluks

An elite body of troops, the Mamluks were recruited from slaves by the Muslims. This late 13th- or early 14th-century bronze bowl shows a mounted Mamluk cavalryman. He holds a curved sabre above his head.

Border of crowns

King on a tile

Medieval churches were often decorated with patterned ceramic tiles. These examples come from Chertsey Abbey, England. They bear a portrait of Richard I, known as Richard the Lionheart, who was king of England from 1189 to 1199.

Mounted Mamluk cavalryman

Arabic inscription

A Saracen

Many Saracens used fast horses and shot arrows at the crusaders. Some wore plate armour, but many wore mail or padded defences. Round shields were common; curved, slashing sabres became popular in the 12th century.

Turkish warrior

This Italian dish, from about 1520, shows a Turkish warrior. The crusades died out in the early 14th century and the great fortified city of Constantinople (modern-day Istanbul) stood between Turkey and mainland Europe. However, the city never fully recovered from the damage it suffered during the Fourth Crusade in 1204.

Fighting for the faith

This picture shows Christians and Muslims clashing in 1218 during the Christian siege of Damietta, Egypt.

Eastern strongholds

The crusaders built stone castles and borrowed ideas from the East. Crusader castles were built on strong natural sites when possible. This castle, Krak des Chevaliers in Syria, was held by the Knights Hospitallers.

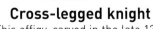

Cross-legged knight

This effigy, carved in the late 13th century, is said to be that of English knight Sir John Holcombe, who died of wounds sustained during the Second Crusade (1147–49).

Knights of Christ

In 1118, a band of knights protected Christian pilgrims in the Holy Land. These men, known as the Knights Templar, became a religious order, but continued to fight the Muslims. In the same period, another order of monks who had worked with the sick became a military order called the Knights of St John, or Knights Hospitaller. After the Christians lost control of the Holy Land in 1291, the Templars disbanded; the Hospitallers moved to the Mediterranean and continued fighting the Muslims.

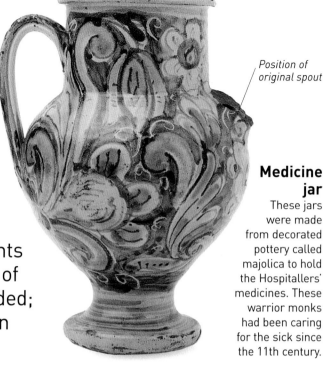

Position of original spout

Medicine jar
These jars were made from decorated pottery called majolica to hold the Hospitallers' medicines. These warrior monks had been caring for the sick since the 11th century.

The hospital
Malta was the final home of the Knights of St John. This 1586 engraving shows them in the great ward of their hospital in the Maltese capital, Valetta.

Bronze mortar
Ingredients for Hospitaller medicines were ground in this mortar.

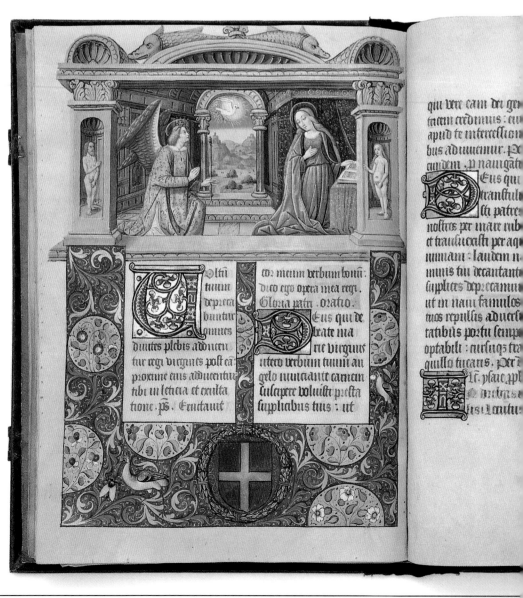

Templars burning

After the Christians took control of the Holy Land, the Templars became very wealthy, but unpopular. The Grand Master, Jacques de Morlay, was burned in 1313 and the Order was suppressed.

Grand Master's seal

This seal belonged to Raymond de Berenger, who ran the Hospitallers from 1363 to 1374.

The fight goes on

After the loss of the Holy Land in 1291, the Hospitallers moved to Cyprus, then to Rhodes in 1310, where they again clashed with the Muslims. Despite their wealth, they avoided the fate of the Templars.

Processional cross

This early 16th-century cross is made of oak covered with silver plate; the figure of Christ is older. The Evangelists are pictured on the arms of the cross, which belonged to the Hospitallers. The coat-of-arms is that of Pierre Decluys, Grand Prior of France from 1522 to 1535.

Order of service

The Knights of St John were expected to attend church and to know their Bible. Breviaries, like the one above, contained the daily service. The religious knights had to obey strict rules, which were usually based on those of the regular monastic orders.

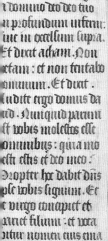

Knight Templar

Templars wore a white surcoat with a red cross. This 12th-century fresco from a Templar church in France shows a knight galloping into battle.

The Rhodes missal

Although skilled warriors, just like other monks the Knights Hospitaller swore to serve the order faithfully, to renounce women, and to help those in need. It is thought that many knights took their vows on this book, the late 15th-century Rhodes missal.

Water bottle

Water was vital in the Mediterranean heat and along pilgrim routes in the Holy Land. This metal water bottle from about 1500 bears the cross of the Order of St John.

Japanese knights

Japan developed a society similar to medieval Europe, and the equivalent of the knight was the samurai. After the Gempei War of 1180–1185, Japan was ruled by an emperor, but real power lay with the military leader, or shogun. Later, civil war weakened the shogun's authority, but a strong shogunate was revived after a victory in 1600, and the last great samurai battle was fought in 1615.

Helmet and face guard
Helmets like this 17th-century example have a neckguard made of iron plates coated with lacquer (a type of varnish) and were laced together with silk.

Early armour
Worn by mounted archers, this 19th-century copy of 12th-century armour (above) is in the great armour, or *O-yoroi*, style. The cuirass is made of small lacquered iron plates.

Tempered edge

Fighting samurai
From the 14th century there was an increase in foot combat, which required new weapons and armour. However, samurai still fought on horseback when necessary.

Swordsman
Samurai prized their swords greatly. In this 19th-century print a samurai is holding his long sword unsheathed. His smaller sword is thrust through his belt.

Pair of swords
The main samurai sword was the *katana*, sheathed in a wooden scabbard (*saya*). The grip (*tsuka*) was covered in rough shark skin to prevent the hand slipping. A pommel cap (*kashira*) fitted over the end. The pair of swords (*daisho*) was completed by a shorter sword (*wakizashi*), which was also stuck through the belt.

Master and servant

This small lacquered case, or *inro*, depicts a servant kneeling before a samurai. Samurai needed servants to attend them and to look after their equipment. A samurai held life-and-death power over his servants and over the farmers who worked on his land and provided him with food.

Modern armour

In a bid to give more protection from bullets, Japanese armour was made more solid from the 16th century. This example is a 19th-century armour called a *tosei gusoku*. A cuirass, or *do*, protects the chest. The helmet (*kabuto*) has a face defence (*mempo*) and is fitted with a buffalo-horn crest.

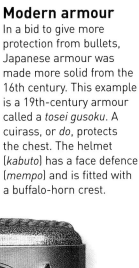

Swordsmanship

In this 19th-century picture, a samurai is instructed in swordplay by creatures called *tengi*. Learning to use the sword correctly took many years of hard work. Japanese swords had extremely sharp cutting edges.

Shark skin grip

Warrior

This 19th-century photograph shows a samurai dressed in his armour. This is made of solid plates of iron, unlike the earlier small, laced plates. Over his armour he wears a surcoat, or *jinbaori*. He carries his swords and a long bow made of bamboo and other woods glued together and bound with rattan. His helmet crest bears a pair of horns.

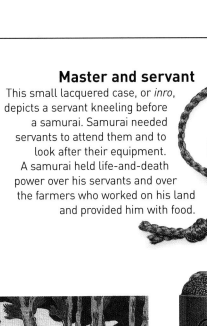

The professionals

Heavily armed squadrons of knights could not break the disciplined ranks of infantry. By 1500, the infantry was becoming the most important part of any army. Feudal forces who fought in return for their land were being replaced by permanent forces of well-trained, paid soldiers. Mounted knights were also becoming less effective on the battlefield.

Grip covered in wood and leather

Crossguard

Lug

Ricasso with leather covering

Flamboyant or wavy edge

Bellows visor

Puffed and slashed armour

In the late 15th and early 16th centuries the Swiss and German foot soldiers, or *Landsknecht*, wore extravagant clothing in the "puffed and slashed" style. This German armour, made in about 1520, mimics that style.

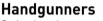

Handgunners

Swiss handgunners of the late 15th century fire matchlock guns at enemy soldiers, backed up by wheeled cannon.

Steel strips to guard inside of elbow

Later mail

Puffed and slashed decoration

Two-handed sword

Swords like this one were useful for cutting the points off pikes carried by enemy soldiers. The lugs on the blade helped prevent an enemy weapon sliding up to the hands. This example dates to about 1600, by which time these were becoming largely ceremonial weapons.

Cat-gutter

This German *Landsknecht*, dating to about 1520, wears partial armour and mail to guard his neck. He carries a two-handed sword and a short sword called a *Katzbalger* (Cat-gutter).

In black and white

Some infantrymen and horsemen chose armour without leg pieces to make walking easier. The open helmet, or burgonet, allowed more air to reach the face. The black and white effect on this armour from about 1550 was made by leaving some areas as bright steel while painting other parts black.

Halberd

The axehead on this weapon from about 1500 could be used to maim an enemy; the beak on the back could trip up horses.

Cheek-piece of burgonet

Halberdier

This *Landsknecht* of the 16th century wears the usual elaborate costume and armour, this time surmounted by a plume. As well as his sword he carries a halberd similar to the one shown on the right.

Gauntlet

German crossbow

When the crossbow bolt struck armour squarely it could punch through it. The crossbow, like this German example from about 1520, was spanned mechanically (pp. 50–51) and could be used more easily than a longbow. They were popular on mainland Europe.

Steel stirrup

Cord and plaited leather binding

Tasset

Bowstring of twisted cord

Gun battery

This woodcut from about 1520 shows a gunner lowering a glowing linstock to the touchhole of a cannon. The barrels have moulded decoration. The increasing use of cannons was one factor in the decline of the castle and the rise of the heavily gunned fortress. Field guns were used against enemies.

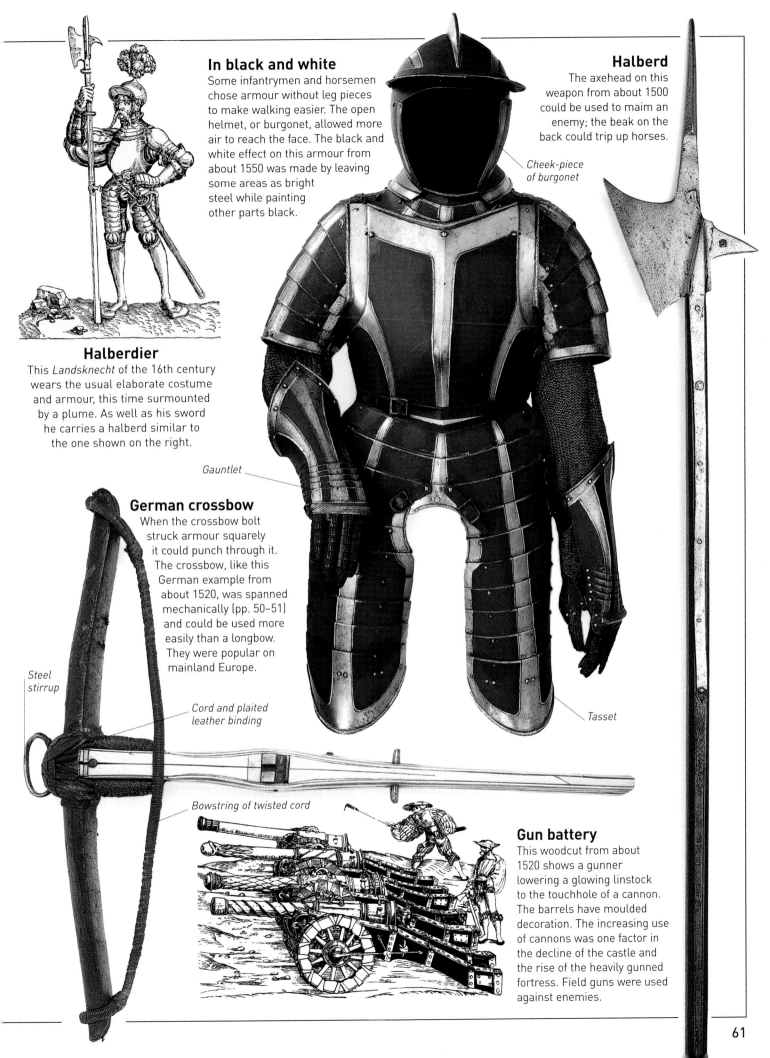

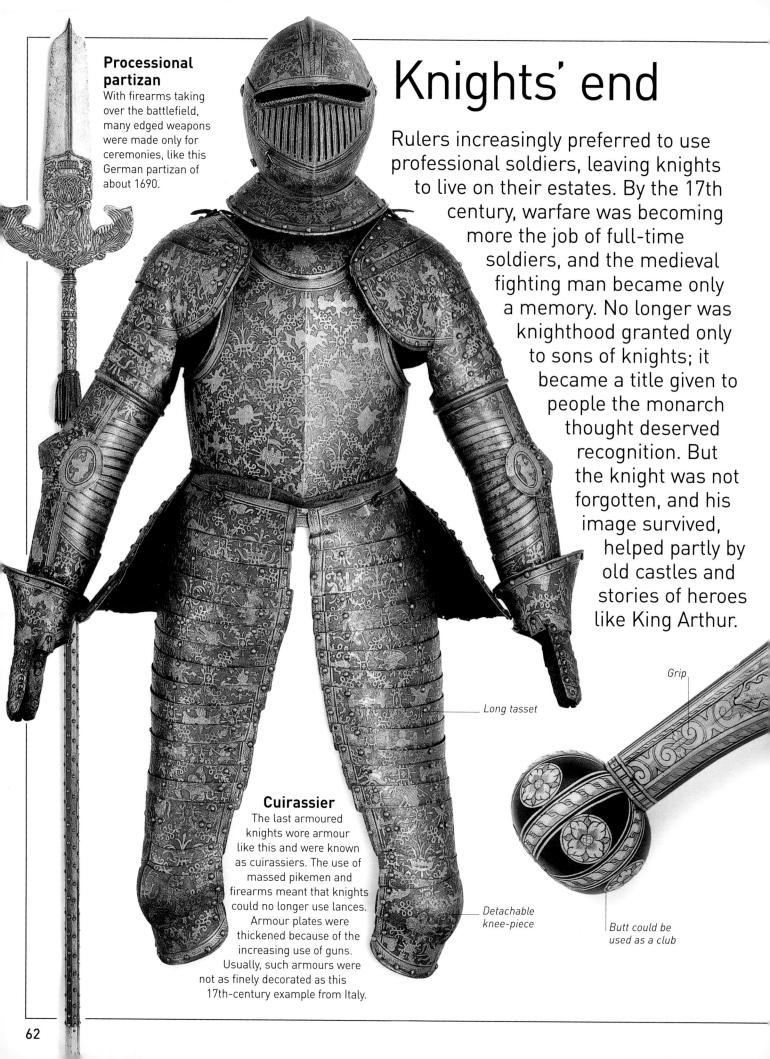

Processional partizan
With firearms taking over the battlefield, many edged weapons were made only for ceremonies, like this German partizan of about 1690.

Knights' end

Rulers increasingly preferred to use professional soldiers, leaving knights to live on their estates. By the 17th century, warfare was becoming more the job of full-time soldiers, and the medieval fighting man became only a memory. No longer was knighthood granted only to sons of knights; it became a title given to people the monarch thought deserved recognition. But the knight was not forgotten, and his image survived, helped partly by old castles and stories of heroes like King Arthur.

Grip

Long tasset

Cuirassier
The last armoured knights wore armour like this and were known as cuirassiers. The use of massed pikemen and firearms meant that knights could no longer use lances. Armour plates were thickened because of the increasing use of guns. Usually, such armours were not as finely decorated as this 17th-century example from Italy.

Detachable knee-piece

Butt could be used as a club

Old versus new

This engraving from 1632 (right) shows how an armoured cuirassier with a lance could be stopped by an infantryman with a musket.

Buff coat

Light cavalrymen found that a coat of buff leather was able to stop a sword cut and was more comfortable than full armour. It was worn either alone or with a breastplate and backplate.

Preparing to fire

An early 17th-century Dutch musketeer (left) pours gunpowder into his musket.

Piece of rock strikes metal to make a spark; this lights the gunpowder and fires the gun

Don Quixote

The Spanish writer Miguel de Cervantes wrote *Don Quixote* in around 1590. A sad yearning for lost chivalry, it tells the story of a foolish man who jousts with windmills and treats a peasant girl as his lady.

Wheel-lock pistol

Cuirassiers and light cavalry carried two wheel-lock pistols. This German example, dating to about 1590, has an ebony stock inlaid with engraved panels and strips of staghorn.

Key cylinder

Ramrod

Screwdriver

Swivel-eye for suspension

Pivoting pricker to unblock vent

Key

This spanner, from about 1620, wound up a spring on the wheel-lock which, when released by the trigger, caused a shower of sparks to fire the gunpowder.

This late 16th-century cartridge-box was designed to hang from a belt

The victor

The chivalrous knight shown is about to receive his prize on this Victorian silhouette. Knightly adventures appealed to the romantic Victorian mind.

Did you know?

AMAZING FACTS

The expression "to get on your high horse" means to be overbearing or arrogant. It comes from the Middle Ages, when people of high rank rode on taller horses than those of lower rank.

During a siege, a trebuchet was sometimes used to throw very unpleasant missiles into a castle, including severed heads, dead animals, and cattle dung.

Krak des Chevalier

Knight's tall horse known as a charger

Knight riding high on horseback

Spiral staircases in medieval castles made life difficult for an attacker fighting his way up, as his weapon (in his right hand) would keep hitting the post in the centre of the stairs.

Due to the damp climate in Japan, samurai armour had to be lacquered to stop it rusting.

The badge of the Knights Templar order was two knights riding on one horse. This represented their original state of poverty.

The name Templars came from their headquarters' location, which was situated near the old Jewish temple in Jerusalem.

King Richard I, known as Richard the Lionheart, ruled England from 1189 to 1199. He was a heroic fighter and zealous crusader, and was committed to the ideal of chivalry.

Pivoting wooden arm

Sling pouch

Trebuchet

Ladders used to scale the city walls

The castle of Krak des Chevaliers in Syria was a crusader castle built in the 12th century. The Knights Hospitaller lived there. The castle was damaged in 2013 during the Syrian Civil War.

Medieval pilgrims wore badges on their hats to show they had been to a shrine.

In 1212, up to 50,000 French and German children took part in a crusade to the Holy Land. Few of them ever returned home. It was called the Children's Crusade.

Castle defenders often dropped missiles onto attackers below. Hot water, red-hot sand, rocks, or quicklime were also used.

The siege of Jerusalem by the Christian crusaders in 1099

QUESTIONS AND ANSWERS

Q What does chivalry mean?

A During the Middle Ages the word chivalry was used to mean the knightly class, who were known as the Chivalry. In time, chivalry came to mean the qualities expected of an ideal knight, such as courtesy, bravery, and honour.

Q Were tournaments dangerous?

A A tournament, or tourney, was a mock battle, but it could be very dangerous and bloody. At one tourney, held in Cologne, Germany, more than 60 knights were killed.

Q What happened to knights who were defeated in battle?

A If a knight defeated an opponent, he would not always kill him. An enemy knight could be more valuable alive than dead, as his family would pay ransom money to get him back.

Q Do knights still exist today?

A Knights in shining armour only exist in museums, but the order of knighthood still remains in Britain. A knighthood is given by the king or queen to a British subject for outstanding service to the country.

Scene from a medieval tournament

Q Who built the first English castle?

A It is hard to know for sure. However, when William of Normandy invaded England in 1066, his soldiers placed fortifications on the old Roman fort at Pevensey. They then may have built a motte and bailey at Hastings, in Sussex, and waited there for the arrival of King Harold and the English army.

Q What were the crusades to the Holy Land?

A The crusades (1095–1291) were a series of holy wars launched by Christian leaders to try and recapture the Holy Land from Muslim control.

Record Breakers

LONGEST RIDE IN ARMOUR
The longest recorded ride in armour was 335 km (208 miles) by Dick Brown. He left Edinburgh on 10 June 1989 and arrived in Dumfries four days later. The total riding time was 35 hours 25 minutes.

THE MOST KNIGHTS
During the reign of Henry II (1154–1189), the king could call upon the services of more than 6,000 knights. Each knight pledged to serve in his army for 40 days each year without pay.

THE MOST EXPENSIVE KING
When Richard I of England was captured by the Duke of Austria in 1192, England paid a ransom of 150,000 marks. This huge sum is equivalent to many millions of pounds today.

Soldiers constructing what could be the first English castle, in 1066

Timeline

In ninth-century Europe, knights fought for their lords. Knightly honour, or chivalry, was born in the 11th century. By the 16th century, armies using pikes and guns replaced the armoured knight. Knights also lived in Japan, and had an impact in other countries, too.

Knight Templar

Knight Hospitaller

- **771–814 Charlemagne employs mounted warriors** Charlemagne, leader of the Franks, and his warriors conquer much of present-day France, Germany, the Low Countries, and Italy.

- **800 Charlemagne is crowned Emperor** On Christmas Day 800, Charlemagne is crowned Emperor of the West by the Pope in Rome. This new empire lasts for more than 1,000 years.

- **814 Charlemagne dies** After the death of Charlemagne, his empire breaks up. Local lords, and those mounted warrior knights who serve them, offer protection to local people in return for labour, giving rise to the feudal system in western Europe.

Wooden spear with iron spearhead

Viking warriors

- **c.850 First castles built** Earth and timber castles are built in France to protect the local lord from his enemies. Castles are also built of stone.

- **911 Normandy founded** Charles III of France gives land to Viking invaders in an attempt to stop them invading his country. The land is called Normandy, "land of the Northmen".

- **1000s The new order of knights** A new social order of mounted, armoured knights develops in parts of western Europe. They serve a local lord or duke and are in turn served by serfs or peasants.

- **1000s Becoming a squire** Many squires are of a lower social class, but later the sons of noble families also become squires. In the 1000s and 1100s, young men who want to become a knight first serve as a squire to a knight.

- **1066 Normans invade England** Duke William of Normandy invades England and defeats King Harold at the Battle of Hastings. William introduces the feudal system into England and builds stone castles.

- **1095 The crusades begin** The Pope launches the first crusade against the Muslim occupation of the Holy Land. Many knights join this army. Further crusades are launched from Europe until Acre, the last Christian stronghold in the Holy Land, is captured by a Muslim army in 1291.

- **1118 Knights Templar formed in Jerusalem** Knights protecting Christian pilgrims in the Holy Land form a religious military order known as the Knights Templar.

- **1100s Added protection** Knights start to add more mail to their armour to protect their arms and legs.

- **1100s The code of chivalry** A code of conduct, known as chivalry, is adopted by all knights. It requires them to behave in a courteous and civil way when dealing with their enemies and places special emphasis on courtly manners towards women.

Mail body armour

A Norman knight

- **1100s The first tournaments** Tournaments, or mock battles, are first fought to train knights for battle. These events take place over a large stretch of countryside.

- **1100s The birth of heraldry** Decorations on shields now become more standardized using a set of rules known as heraldry. This increasingly elaborate system enables a knight to be identified by the symbols on his shield, or by his full coat-of-arms.

• **1100s New siege machines** The first trebuchets – pivoting sling catapults – are used in siege warfare in western Europe. They join existing weapons, such as catapults, battering rams, and ballistas (large, mounted crossbows) in besieging and attacking castles.

• **1100s Age of the troubadours** Troubadours, or minstrels, from southern France popularize poems of courtly love, romance, and chivalry. Stories about King Arthur and his knights of the round table become increasingly popular throughout western Europe.

• **1185 Shogun, Japan** A samurai warrior class led by the Shogun, or military leader, takes power in Japan, although the emperor is still the official ruler of the country.

• **1189–1199 Richard I** Richard Coeur de Lion, nicknamed "the Lionheart", rules England. He fights in the third crusade, from 1190 to 1192, and is a prisoner from 1192 to 1194.

• **1190 The Teutonic Knights** This new religious and military order of knights is formed to fight in the crusades, but soon focuses on converting pagans to Christianity in eastern Europe.

• **1200s Added horsepower** Most knights have two warhorses, as well as a destrier for jousting, a sumpter, or packhorse, for carrying baggage, and a palfrey for arduous long journeys.

• **1200s Safer tournaments** Blunted weapons are introduced to make the tournaments safer. A new form of contest – jousts – is also introduced, in which two knights fight on horseback with lances or sometimes swords.

• **1200s The rising cost of knighthood** The cost of becoming a knight is so expensive that many young men avoid being knighted and remain as squires. In later years, the word squire comes to mean a gentleman who owns land.

• **1280s New weapons** Pointed swords replace double-edged cutting swords. They can be thrust between the plates of armour that knights now wear to protect themselves.

• **1300s New plated armour** Knights now begin to add steel plates to their armour to protect their body further. They also wear a coat-of-plates, made of pieces of iron riveted to a cloth.

Edward the Black Prince, English hero of the Battle of Crécy

• **1300s The arrival of cannons** Cannons now appear on the battlefield to replace battering rams, catapults, and other manual machines for sieges.

• **1300s Jousting on foot** Combat between two knights on foot becomes popular at tournaments. The knights use swords and are allowed a set number of blows. By the 1400s, such contests have developed into more complex events involving javelins and axes as well as swords.

• **1300s Defence against the knight** In 1302, Flemish footsoldiers using clubs defeat French mounted knights at the Battle of Courtrai. In 1314, Scottish spear formations using pikes stop a charge by English mounted knights and defeat them at the Battle of Bannockburn. Both battles prove that knights are not invincible.

• **1337–1453 The Hundred Years' War** In 1337, Edward III of England claims the French throne and invades the country. War between the two countries continues on and off for more than 100 years. Thanks to their longbowmen, the English achieve victories over French knights at Crécy (1346), Poitiers (1356), and Agincourt (1415).

• **1400 Full body armour** Knights begin to wear full suits of plate armour, giving them all-over body protection.

• **1476–1477 France v Burgundy** War between France and Burgundy shows how mounted knights are unable to defeat solid bodies of pikemen backed up by soldiers using handguns.

• **1494 France invades Italy** France's invasion of Italy in 1494 leads to a long power struggle in Europe between France and the Hapsburg empire of Spain and Austria.

• **1500s Designer armour** Knights still wearing armour etch designs into the metal with acid; gold plating is sometimes used.

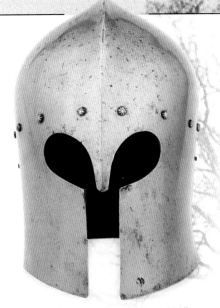

Italian barbute or iron helmet, 1445

• **1500s A professional army** Paid armies of well-trained soldiers, backed up by mercenaries and locally recruited men, gradually replace the feudal armies of previous years. Knights now play a less effective role in battle.

• **1517 The Reformation** In Germany Martin Luther starts a revolt against the Roman Catholic Church that leads to the creation of Protestant churches throughout western Europe.

• **1600s The end of the tournament** During the 1600s, the tournament is replaced in most countries by displays of horsemanship, called carousels.

• **1600s The end of an era** As warfare becomes the job of full-time soldiers and mercenaries, the era of chivalrous knights comes to an end.

Martin Luther preaching for a reformed Church in Germany

Find out more

There are many ways that you can find out more about knights. Some of the best museums and castles are listed on the opposite page. Your local library and bookshop will also have plenty of books for you to read about knights, and there are often programmes and films on television and video for you to watch at home. Above all, check out the Internet – some of the best websites to visit are listed below – and you too will soon become a dedicated knight-watcher.

Design a coat-of-arms

You can design your own or your family's coat-of-arms and use it to decorate your personal letters and belongings. The symbols you choose should be something special to you or have some connection to your name or to the place where you live.

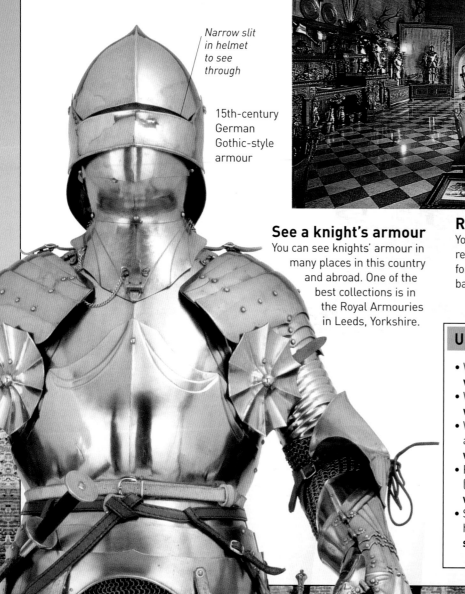

The Great Hall, Warwick Castle

Narrow slit in helmet to see through

15th-century German Gothic-style armour

See a knight's armour

You can see knights' armour in many places in this country and abroad. One of the best collections is in the Royal Armouries in Leeds, Yorkshire.

Return to medieval times

You can see how knights lived and fought in dramatic reconstructions of medieval life. In Warwick Castle, for example, you can see how a knight prepared for battle, and the magnificent Great Hall.

USEFUL WEBSITES

- Website for the Royal Armouries
  www.armouries.org.uk
- Website for the Tower of London
  www.hrp.org.uk/webcode/tower_home.asp
- Website for Warwick Castle, containing information about the castle, jousting, and other events held there
  www.warwick-castle.co.uk
- For a virtual tour of the British Museum's collection (in search field, type in "armour" or "medieval")
  www.britishmuseum.org/explore.aspx
- Samurai collection showcasing suits of armour, helmets, masks, weapons, and horse equipment
  samuraicollection.org/mac/index_web.html

Visit a medieval castle

Visit a medieval castle and see how it was built to withstand attack from an enemy or used to keep the local population under control. You can also usually walk on the ramparts, explore the knights' living quarters, and see the kitchens in which the food was prepared.

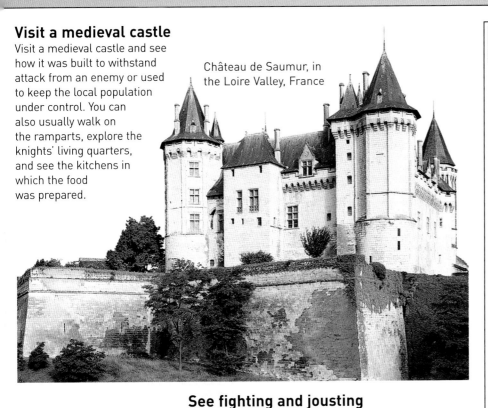

Château de Saumur, in the Loire Valley, France

See fighting and jousting

Some historical re-enactment groups put on displays of fighting or jousting today. Look in the useful websites box on the opposite page for more details. If you are lucky, you could even see a full-scale re-enactment of a medieval tournament.

Sir Galahad is introduced to King Arthur and the knights of the round table

King Arthur

Modern-day jouster charges his opponent with a lance

Stories of King Arthur

You can read stories about knights in the tales of the legendary King Arthur and his knights of the round table. There is still dispute about who King Arthur was, or whether he actually existed at all, but most people now believe that he was a British chieftain or warrior who led the resistance to the Saxon invasion of England in the fifth or sixth centuries.

PLACES TO VISIT

THE ROYAL ARMOURIES, LEEDS

A national museum that tells the story of arms and armour from around the world. Star attractions include:
- Two of the suits of armour belonging to King Henry VIII
- About 500 pieces of archery equipment

WARWICK CASTLE

A medieval castle that is also one of the finest stately homes in England. The main sights include:
- 14th-century ramparts and towers
- The armoury, which features a massive 14th-century, two-hand sword

THE TOWER OF LONDON

This is the medieval fortress on the River Thames. Among the attractions here are:
- The White Tower, commissioned by William the Conqueror in 1078
- The Crown Jewels, which include the crowns, sceptres, and orbs

OTHER MEDIEVAL CASTLES TO VISIT: LEEDS CASTLE, KENT
- A continuously inhabited castle ever since it was built in the 12th century

ROCHESTER CASTLE, KENT
- Vast Norman castle with a commanding great tower surrounded by huge walls

BODIAM CASTLE, EAST SUSSEX
- 14th-century castle with a tower at each corner surrounded by a moat

CAERPHILLY CASTLE, SOUTH WALES
- Fine example of a concentric castle surrounded by water and outer walls

CAERNARFON CASTLE, NORTH WALES
- Begun by Edward I in 1283, this vast castle symbolized the conquest of Wales by the English king

EDINBURGH CASTLE, SCOTLAND
- Massive fortress, garrison, and one-time royal palace

CHATEAU DE SAUMUR, FRANCE
- A 14th-century castle that towers over the town of Saumur on the River Loire

CHATEAU-GAILLARD, FRANCE
- Ruins of the massive castle built by Richard the Lionheart on a cliff

Glossary

BALLISTA A weapon used in siege warfare, consisting of a giant crossbow that shot bolts.

BARBARIANS Uncivilized people. The word is often used to describe the tribes who invaded the Roman Empire in the 4th–5th centuries CE.

BATTLEMENT The top of a castle wall with gaps in it, through which archers could shoot at enemies.

BIT The metal part of a bridle that fits inside the horse's mouth and is used to control the horse.

BODKIN A long, thin arrowhead, shaped like a needle.

Bodkin

BOLT An arrow used for shooting from a weapon, such as a crossbow.

BUTT A target set on a mound of earth, used by archers for shooting practice.

CATAPULT A device to launch missiles.

CHALICE A cup used to hold the wine in the Christian service of mass, or the holy communion.

CHIVALRY Originally meaning good horsemanship, chivalry came to refer to qualities expected of an ideal knight, such as courage, honour, courtesy and, later, courtly manners towards women.

COAT-OF-ARMS A set of symbols used by a knight on his shield or surcoat to identify him in battle or at a tournament.

COAT-OF-PLATES A form of body armour consisting of many pieces of iron riveted to a cloth covering.

CRENEL A gap on the top part of a castle wall, through which defenders could shoot at attackers.

CROSSBOW A bow fixed across a wooden handle with a groove for a bolt. A cord was then released to shoot the bolt.

CRUSADES A series of military expeditions made by European knights during the Middle Ages. The aim of the crusades was to capture the Holy Land from Muslim control.

DESTRIER A knight's warhorse.

DUBBING The ceremony at which a squire was made a knight.

EFFIGY A sculpture of a person.

EMBRASURE An alcove set in a castle wall with a small opening through which archers, crossbowmen, or gunners could shoot.

ETCHING Using acid to "eat" a design onto exposed parts of metal. Suits of armour were often etched with patterns.

FEUDAL SYSTEM A social system used in Europe in the Middle Ages, whereby a local lord gave land to his vassals in return for their allegiance and service.

GARRISON A group of soldiers stationed in a castle or town to defend it.

GATEHOUSE The entrance to a castle, often protected with heavily fortified towers, a portcullis, drawbridge, and a ditch or moat outside.

GILDING Putting a thin covering of gold on an object to decorate it.

HERALDRY A system of using symbols on knights' shields or coats-of-arms so that they could be easily identified in battle or in tournaments.

HERETIC Someone whose religious views are unacceptable to the mainstream church.

HOLY GRAIL According to legend, the Holy Grail was the cup that Jesus used at the Last Supper. In the stories of King Arthur, many of his knights went on quests to find the Holy Grail.

INFANTRY Soldiers who fought on foot.

JOUST A combat between two mounted knights armed with lances.

KEEP A castle's stone tower, probably used for storage or as living quarters.

Gatehouse to Caerphilly Castle, Wales

KNIGHT A warrior who fought on horseback. The term is normally used for the period c.800–1600, when warriors fought with swords and lances.

KNIGHTS HOSPITALLER A military order of monks who also cared for the sick. They were also known as the Knights of St John.

KNIGHTS TEMPLAR An order of monks who were also fighting knights. They fought against the Muslims and protected Christian pilgrims in the Holy Land.

LANCE A long weapon with a wooden shaft and a pointed metal head. Knights used lances when they were charging on horseback.

LONGBOW A large bow used during the Middle Ages. It was usually made of yew wood and could shoot arrows up to 300 m (984 ft) away.

Embrasure in a castle wall

Joust at Tours in France, 1446

LUGS Two small cross-pieces on a spear or sword that stopped the weapon being pushed too far into an opponent's body and getting stuck.

MACE A heavy weapon, consisting of a metal head on top of a wooden pole.

MAIL A form of armour made of many small, linked iron rings. Mail could be made up into garments, such as coats.

MERCENARY A hired soldier who fought simply for money.

MOOR A Muslim from northwest Africa.

MOTTE AND BAILEY An early style of castle. The motte was a mound with a wooden tower on top; the bailey was a courtyard below the motte that contained the domestic buildings.

NORMANS People who came from Normandy in northern France. The Normans were descended from the Vikings who settled in the region during the 10th century. In 1066, the Normans conquered England under their leader, Duke William of Normandy.

PAGE A young boy servant in the household of a king or great knight. He was in training to become a knight.

Re-enactment of Japanese feudal lords paying their respects to the Shogun

Model of a Japanese samurai

PALFREY A horse used for very long journeys.

PEASANT A farm labourer or other person who works for a lord.

PILGRIMAGE A journey to a sacred place for religious reasons. In the Middle Ages, some Christians went on pilgrimages to Jerusalem and to other sites in the Holy Land.

PLATE ARMOUR Body armour made of large metal pieces, as opposed to mail.

POMMEL A round knob on the end of a sword handle, which helped to balance the weight of the blade.

PORTCULLIS A metal gate, or an iron-clad wooden gate, which could be lowered in front of the entrance to a castle to stop attackers getting in.

QUIVER A bag hung from an archer's back, or more usually his waist, in which he stored his arrows.

RANSOM A sum of money demanded for the release of a prisoner captured or defeated in battle. The captors demanded the ransom from the prisoner's family.

SAMURAI A Japanese warrior.

SARACEN A name used at the time of the crusades for all Muslims and Arabs.

SCALING LADDER A long ladder used by attacking soldiers to try to climb over the wall of a castle.

SCONCE A candlestick for hanging on a wall.

SERF A labourer who was not allowed to leave the land on which he worked.

SHOGUN A Japanese military leader.

SHRINE A holy site, like a saint's tomb.

SPUR A spiked device that a knight fitted to his heels to urge his horse forwards.

SQUIRE A young man who served a knight, and was training to become one.

Spur

STIRRUPS Two loops suspended from a horse's saddle to support the rider's feet.

SURCOAT A loose coat or robe worn over armour. It was sometimes decorated with his coat-of-arms.

TILT A barrier used in jousting to separate the knights and avoid collisions.

TOURNAMENT A pageant that included mock battles, jousting, and foot combat, in which knights practised their fighting

TREBUCHET A weapon used in sieges to throw large missiles at a castle.

TROUBADOURS Medieval French poets who composed and sang poems on the theme of courtly love.

VISOR The moveable part of a helmet that covered the face.

WINDLASS A machine with a horizontal axle, used to wind back catapults and ballistas, as well as some later powerful crossbows.

Index

Acknowledgements

Dorling Kindersley would like to thank:
The Wallace Collection, the Royal Armouries, the British Museum, and the Museum of the Order of St John, for provision of objects for photography; English Heritage, the National Trust, and Cadw (Welsh Historical Monuments), for permission to photograph at Rochester, Bodiam, & Caerphilly castles; David Edge for information on items in the Wallace Collection; Paul Cannings, Jonathan Waller, John Waller, Bob Dow, Ray Monery, & Julia Harris for acting as models; Anita Burger for make-up; Joanna Cameron for illustrations (pages 22–23); Angels & Burmans for costumes.

For this edition, the publisher would also like to thank: the author for assisting with revisions; Claire Bowers, David Ekholm-JAlbum, Sunita Gahir, Joanne Little, Nigel Ritchie, Susan St Louis, Carey Scott, & Bulent Yusuf for the clipart; David Ball, Neville Graham, Rose Horridge, Joanne Little, & Sue Nicholson for the wallchart; BCP, Marianne Petrou, & Owen Peyton Jones for checking the digitized files.

The publisher would like to thank the following for their kind permission to reproduce their images:
(Key: a-above; b-below/bottom; c-center; f-far; l-left; r-right; t-top)

Ancient Art & Architecture Collection: 58cl, 58c, 58tr, 59bl, 65b.
Board of the Trustees of the Armouries: 70tl.
Bridgeman Art Library, London/New York: 53b/Biblioteca Estense, Modena: 10b/Bibliotheque de L'Arsenal, Paris: 64br/British Library: 19c, 20tr, 20c, 38cr, 39c, 49tr, 54tl/Bibliotheque Municipal de Lyon: 55c/ Bibliotheque Nationale, Paris: 11br, 15tr, 22cr, 25tl, 41tr, 42bl, 43t, 54bl, 57tr/Corpus Christi College, Cambridge: 13rc/Corpus Christi College, Oxford: 54br/Musee Conde, Chantilly: 50bl, 51bl, 65t/ Vatican Library, Rome: 50br/ Victoria & Albert Museum: 37cl/Wrangham Collection: 59c.
British Museum: 71cr.
Burgerbibliothek, Bern: 25rc.
Christ Church, Oxford/Photo: Bodleian Library: 27tl.
Dorling Kindersley: Photo from Children just Like Me by Barnabus & Anabel Kindersley, published by DK: 71bl.
E.T. Archive: 6bl, 11tl, 18bl, 27tr, 30bl, 31bl, 33cl, 33cr, 39tr, 41c, 49bl, 57bc, 58cc, 59c, 60c/British Library: 19bc, 32c/ British Museum: 27bl/ Fitzwilliam Museum, Cambridge: 48rc.
Mary Evans Picture Library: 69bl.
Robert Harding Picture Library: 8tl, 12rc, 18tr, 22bl, 26c, 34br, 34bl, 55bl/British Library: 11c, 34cl, 44b, 45bl.
Heritage Images: British Library 46bl.
Michael Holford: 8bl, 9tr, 52c, 55br.
Hulton-Deutsch Collection: 56cl.
A.F. Kersting: 9cl.

Mansell Collection: 11bl, 21c, 39tr, 46br, 55tl, 63bl/Alinari: 46tr.
Bildarchiv Foto Marburg: 48br.
Arxiu Mas: 54cl.
Stadtbibliothek Nurnberg: 17rc.
Osterreichische Nationalbibliotehek, Vienna (Cod.2597, f.15): 40br.
Pierpont Morgan Library, New York: 29c.
Scala: 7br, 33t, 34tlc, 36cl.
Stiftsbibliothek St Gallen: 6c.
Syndication International: 26br, 27cl, 27tcl, 32bc, 37tl, 41tl, 50tr, 53t, 57tl/Photo Trevor Wood: 36tr.
Warwick Castle: 68cb.

Wallchart:
DK Images: Judith Miller / Otford Antiques and Collectors Centre 1bl (Brooch); Judith Miller / Sloan's 1tr; Michael Holford: 1clb (Pilgrimage).

All other images © Dorling Kindersley

For further information see:
www.dkimages.com